Dancing – Thinking

Pierre Petiot

Dancing - Thinking

I stretched ropes from bell tower to bell tower; garlands from window to window; gold chains from star to star, and I dance.

Arthur Rimbaud

The pretext of the following text is a conference by Paul Valéry delivered on March 5, 1936 at the *Université des Annales* and published in *Conferencia* in November 1936. The text used here is that of the version published by *Allia Editions* in 2023 under the title *Philosophie de la Danse*.

We can only hope that Valéry's few introductory words may be applied here:

> "You must resign yourself to hearing some proposals that a man who does not dance is going to risk in front of you about dancing. You will wait a little for the moment of wonder, and you will say to yourself that I am no less impatient than you to be delighted with it.
>
> I immediately enter into my ideas, and I tell you without further preparation that Dance, in my opinion, is not limited to being an exercise, an entertainment, an ornamental art, or sometimes a parlor game; it is a serious thing and, in certain aspects, a very venerable thing."

Hence, like Valéry, let's get into the ideas right away!

> Ants don't waste a minute. The spider watches and does not play on its web. But man? Man is this singular animal who watches himself live, who gives himself a value, and who places all this value that he is pleased to give himself in the importance he attaches to useless perceptions and to actions without vital, physical consequences.

Paul Valéry – *Philosophie de la danse* – P16

Valéry supposes – invents – that animals would be perpetually busy with their survival… The same was said of prehistoric men, before the book *Stone Age Economics* by Marshall Sahlins came to bring economists

back to observation and to reason… Rather than their blind confidence in tales from the Holy Bible. A few ethnographic observations might have sufficed, if economists had been able to take the trouble to *observe* before pontificating on subjects that they knew nothing about. Moreover, little moved by the facts, we still see almost everywhere that they persevere spreading over the entire world, a rarity that they are working hard to set up.
As for ants, we now know how things really are, and what La Fontaine could hardly have known: ants give the impression of always being at work, but this is only an impression. They walk around and roam a lot, and are not that hardworking.

Man is therefore in no way this artisan of the useless, this exception within the living world that thereby attempts to elevate himself beyond the condition of other animals. Obsessed by so-called *natural selection* – in most cases a phantasmagorical representation of capitalist competition – most people, scientists included sometimes even, seem to have forgotten that, for there to be natural selection, there must have been *natural creation* beforehand, otherwise selection would have stopped a long time ago, for lack of characteristics to select.

> "They always tell us about Dar-win, but they never tell us anything about Dar-lose" once joked a friend…

Actually, the creative capacities of living things exceed by far the useful. And that is fortunate. Because what is useful is only identifiable based on circumstances, either present or foreseeable in the short term. But in the longer term, on the scale of a few million years, circumstances very quickly exceed human capacities for prediction and anticipation... However, as everyone can see, even over millions of years, the circumstances in no way exceed the creative capacities of living things, taken as a global system, that is to say beyond the particular case of each species. Because life has been lasting for around 3.5 billion years, an order of magnitude of duration which is far beyond the imagination of human beings.

Life, no more than men themselves – whatever they say about it – does not know in the least where it is going. It only gets out of trouble through unbridled creativity, the majority of which is statistically likely to be of no use, and only a tiny part of which could prove useful, on occasion, for possible adaptations. And therefore, if man, like everything else in life, is in fact an artisan of the useless, this, as we have just seen, in no way disqualifies the useless, on the contrary.

> [...] this thought which edifies us, in our own eyes, above our sensitive condition, is exactly the thought which serves no purpose. [...] Our deepest thoughts are the most indifferent to our preservation and, in a way, futile in relation to it.
> Paul Valéry – *Philosophie de la danse* – P17

Well, "indifferent to our conservation"? From what point of view? With respect to which time scales? And, as for our conservation, is it the conservation of individuals or that of the species? All utilitarian thinking is necessarily short-term thinking, short-sighted thinking, since the long and very long term are unimaginable, that is to say beyond the reach of any thinking. Therefore, "The thought that is of no use", far from being nothing more than a monstrous waste – which it obviously also is – constitutes in fact, although perhaps infinitesimally from a statistical point of view, our only hope of long-term survival, in that it attempts to go beyond even the imaginable. This wandering, this truly insane risk, this excursion of the living beyond the immediately useful, in short, this incredible *expense* and *luxury*, is in fact at the heart of this strange ability to go on living which carries us and all of life.

Of course, what, with a little hindsight and distance, through the diversity of circumstances and species, appears to us as a sort of creativity orgy of the living, is only valid insofar as it is not opposed to the fundamental necessity of reproduction, to the diversity of characteristics accumulated within each individual, as well as within each species, nor to the accumulation of the diversity of species required to cope with the diversity of circumstances.

> But our curiosity, more avid than is necessary, and our activity more excitable than any vital goal requires, has developed to the invention of the arts, of the sciences, of universal problems, and to the invention of the production of objects, forms, actions, which we could easily do without.
>
> Paul Valéry – *Philosophie de la danse* – P17

Valéry glimpses – almost – the biological necessity of the uselessness when he considers curiosity, a much more than human faculty, of which he knows well that animals are obviously not deprived. As he also knows well that all curiosity, whether animal or human, is by very definition of curiosity, in excess, that is to say more eager than is necessary. And that's even how we recognize it. But instead of understanding human curiosity as the – no doubt hypertrophied – extension of a prior underlying animal curiosity, of an animal curiosity resulting from biological evolution and from which human curiosity as such emerges, otherwise incomprehensible and as if "fallen from Heavens", Valéry focuses (and rightly so!) on the fundamental, radical uselessness of civilizations themselves and their products, "which we could easily do without".

Why do we devote ourselves so ardently to the production of objects, of shapes and actions that we could easily do without? This is by virtue of another aspect to which Valéry often returns – and to which it will indeed be necessary to return – which is the truly addictive character of intellectual creativity.

> Art like science, each according to its own way, tends to make a sort of useful out of the useless, a sort of necessary, out of the arbitrary. Thus, artistic creation is not so much a creation of works as it is a creation of the need for works [...]

Philosophie de la danse – P17-18

If we agree – with reluctance and very temporarily – to accept the separation that Valéry establishes between the producer and the consumer of intellectual creativity (in his *Cours de Poétique* at Collège de France), then we must consider the addiction caused through intellectual creativity according to these two sides, that of production and that of consumption. And in this perspective, dance appears, to Valéry as to us, as a very pure example of the producer's addiction process, whose movement escapes what we call reality, that is to say any *commonly agreed upon* understanding of the Real.

> [...] the dancer is in another world, which is no longer the one that is painted with our gaze, but the one that she weaves with her steps and constructs with her gestures. But, in this world, there is no external goal to actions; there is no object to seize, to join or to push away or to flee, an object which exactly completes an action and gives to the movements, first, an external direction and coordination, and then a clear and certain conclusion.

Philosophie de la danse – P27-28

Certainly the movement of the dancer escapes any goal external to that – in actions – of the body and mind of the dancer, but Valéry by the same movement reveals to us a secret that only the mathematicians who created the new conceptions of geometry towards the end of the 19th century – such as *Henri Poincaré* – could have revealed to us if we had had the audacity to read them. A secret which is that space is not this infinite and empty continuum that Newton (and more generally the 17th century) created ex-nihilo, but that, on the contrary, it is *defined* (*constructed*) by the groups of *transformations* (i.e. rotations, translations, etc...) which operate in it.

In other words, space is not anything given in itself. It is nothing such as a sort of pre-existing theater setting within which our life and our gestures would be inscribed, but that – at an intuitive level at least – it is, at the opposite woven and constructed by our actions and gestures. (See Chapter 3, *Pourquoi l'espace a 3 dimensions* in *Dernières Pensées,* Henri Poincaré – Flammarion 1913-1917). More precisely, Poincaré shows that our intuition of space is essentially based on the notion of movement. On the internal – muscular – perception of the *movements* of our body.
This is an approach that makes Marx's words resonate somewhat strangely: in the dynamics of dance, the difference between interpretation and transformation collapses because the space, invoked and then created by the movement of the dancer, finds itself *simultaneously interpreted and transformed* – more precisely, interpreted *because* transformed by the dancer's actions. This reveals to us that the meaning of the word *interpretation* in Marx's sentence was only aimed at an *abstract* interpretation, that is to say non-physically experienced, and hence in a certain way as we will suggest later, not-danced.

Henri Poincaré explains that space is not this empty absolute that Newton spoke of, but that it is essentially *relative*:

> By this I mean, not only that we could be transported to another region of space without realizing it (and this is indeed what happens since we do not notice the translation of the Earth), not only that all the dimensions of objects could be increased in the same proportion, without our being able to know it, provided that our measuring instruments participate in this enlargement; but I also want to say that space could be deformed according to an arbitrary law, provided that our measuring instruments are deformed precisely according to the same law

Henri Poincaré, *Dernières Pensées*, P61-62

And he specifies right after that what he means by "arbitrary law" is a continuous distortion...

> Space, considered independently of our measuring instruments, therefore has neither metric nor projective properties; it only has topological properties. It is amorphous, that is to say that it does not differ from that which one would deduce from any continuous deformation.

Henri Poincaré, *Dernières Pensées*, P62

We immediately sense how close this vision of space conceived *as essentially deformable* is to that of the *deformable* space-time of the *Theory of Relativity* – in the development of which Poincaré also largely participated.

Poincaré therefore explains to us that there exists something underlying the usual space, something deeper, which is what allows the mathematician to reason correctly even based on poorly made figures (*Dernières Pensées*, P59-70), which is the field that the discipline of mathematics that is now called *Topology* studies, and which turns out to be the study of an amorphous space, that is to say without shapes – since it can be deformed at will.

But then, returning to Valéry's dancer, the question arises of the nature of the material prior to the creation of the space that the dancer weaves and constructs with her steps and gestures. It is obviously not a matter of a space, since the space is precisely the dancer who creates it.

We still live, for the most part of us, with the idea - ultimately rather incongruous - of an infinite space, without suspecting what this representation can have as *religious*, that is to say, as specifically *terrorist*. As evidenced by this anguished revelation from Blaise Pascal, on the back of his theological wanderings, "the eternal silence of these infinite spaces frightens me...". To which, the thought of the good Gaston Bachelard responds without trembling: "I do not live in infinity, because in infinity, one is not at home". Revealing thereby that the role, the function, of all these infinities had in fact no other reason to exist than to drive us out of our homes, out of *our world*. To make us *permanent strangers*.

In the new geometry that both mathematics and dance reveal to us, on the other hand, we are ineradicably at home since it is our movements and our actions that weave and construct a space, beyond which there can only be what Anaximander called *Apeiron*, "devoid of perimeter" (the two terms share the same etymological root "peri")), that is to say an *indeterminate*, an *indefinite*, but *not an unlimited* in the usual sense of the word. Of course, taken literally, *unlimited* means without limits, but it then means *a lack of limit*, which has nothing to do with any kind of infinity. If my neighbor's land has not been demarcated, it is correct to say that my neighbor's land is without boundaries, limitless. But no one will conclude from this that it is *unlimited* in the sense of *infinite*. If, moreover, as a result of an oversight, my neighbor's land does not even appear in the land register, then it is *indeterminate, indefinite*, but it is not thereby infinite. If we translate "rigorously", "literally", the word *Apeiron* by *unlimited* in the usual sense of *unlimited*, then reversibly, I have the right to claim that if God is infinite, it is *because He is not completely finished*, which will probably earn me the ire of most theologians.

In other words, *Apeiron* does not mean unlimited or infinite. Infinity which, moreover, everywhere and always, never reveals itself as anything other than the endless repetition of the same.

And then, unless we make the culture of ignorance a method suitable for exploring the mysteries of the Real, it has become intellectually dishonest not to take into account the findings of the mathematician Georg Cantor, according to which there are different kinds of infinities, large ones and small ones, which we can somehow nest into each other... Thus the set of natural integers is infinite in its particular way (countable), but it can be included – and it is generally included – in the set of real numbers, which is also infinite, but in a different and completely singular way, since the set of real numbers included (for example) between 0 and 1 is no less infinite than the set of all real numbers taken in their totality, which can seem quite dizzying.

But we are not at the end of our vertigo, as Cantor also shows that there are no more elements in a space of dimension N (N being a finite integer) than in real numbers between 0 and 1 (or in the whole set of real numbers). Confronted with this (mathematical) evidence, Cantor was so surprised by his discovery that he wrote: "I see it, but I don't believe it! ".

What Cantor's discoveries reveal in this case is that when we talk about a space of dimension N, we are only ever talking about a particular *structuring* of an infinite set of elements whose number n is "not greater" than the number of elements of a space of dimension 1. But a space of dimension 1, such as, for example, the set of real numbers itself, only corresponds to a particular structuring (the axioms structure that *makes* the real numbers) of an infinite set, say, "of a large size" – of a size greater in any case than the size of the infinite set of natural integers.

But these different structures are *constraints* (as pataphysicists would say), which determine, define *forms* inside, or rather *out of*, the Apeiron. Forms which allow us in some way to explore some little bits of what *emerges out of the Apeiron*. Out of, but neither *in*, nor *from* the Apeiron, since Anaximander' *apeiron*, has neither determined forms nor qualities.

In short, the mathematical dancer proceeds in the same way as Valéry's dancer. She makes gestures (she develops axioms, definitions, demonstrations, theorems), *gestures of thought*, of course, but gestures all the same, and these gestures weave and construct … Not the space, of course not, but mathematics.

In Anaximander's vision, it is the Apeiron itself which, at any moment, *is* the activity which *generates* all forms, mineral, vegetable or animal. Humans – and their creations – are just a particular case.

Hence, rather than following Heidegger's meanderings, while partly – and joyfully – betraying Anaximander, we will here prefer to interpret *Apeiron* from the Chinese point of view of the *Tao*, as *this indeterminate from which all forms are emancipated.* Or, if we prefer things that way, under the trappings of the quantum vacuum, which is just as creative as the Tao is said to be. Or even as this *Mouth of Shadow* that Victor Hugo speaks of in *Les Contemplations*.

And this is what allows Valéry to compare dance and dreams and to say about the dancer in action…

Nothing exists beyond the system that she forms for herself through her actions, a system which makes us think of the completely opposite and no less closed system that sleep constitutes for us, whose completely opposite law is the abolition, total abstention of any acts.

Philosophie de la Danse - P 29

A remark where Valéry's repugnance regarding dreams can be sensed. *Dream...* A word that Valery takes here great care to circumvent by rather referring to sleep. A wasted effort however, since neither sleep nor dreams exhibit a total abstention from actions. And it is enough to observe the surreptitious movements that a dreaming cat or dog makes, or even more simply those of the next human sleeper at hand, to grasp what very strangely lacks here in Valéry conceptions, and which is the understanding of the mind as *a simulating activity*.

Because we now know – and scientifically – that neither movements nor actions are absent from dreams. We know that they are present in dreams, as *simulated* and *inhibited*, and that they sometimes happen to escape into reality, out of sleep and out of dreams, out of this supposed total abstention from actions, that Valéry speaks of.

Yet, in fact, what seems to be at the heart of Valéry's above remark is rather the idea of a *closure*, of a dynamic of the dancer which *closes* on the *system* that she forms for herself through her actions. So that what this closure designates is this Apeiron that constitutes the *beyond* of her movements. An indeterminate and an indefinite which is not even made of space, since space is what the dancer's actions weave and construct at every moment, and since her movements have not yet determined and defined anything out of this Apeiron, which thus appears as what it is: *an absence of space*.

But this *system* that the dancer forms for herself leads us to another Apeiron. Because this system that the dancer forms, must itself come from some other indeterminate, from some other indefinite, *an internal one*, whose moires appear, evolve, and disappear at any moment within the body and mind of the dancer, and which constitute the very source of her actions. So that if, armed with Mallarmé's *Coup de Dés*, we admit that "*toute pensée émet un coup de dés*", we must then admit that the same is true of the actions of the dancer that, no less than our thoughts do, only emerge and stand out against *a background of chance.* So that,

13

to the external Apeiron we already identified, we must now add another Apeiron, another indeterminate, *an internal indefinite* this time.
And, from the point where we now stand, through the mental intermediary of a Klein Bottle – a well-known object whose interior is also its exterior – we can come to suspect that in this matter, the external Apeiron and the internal Apeiron are one.

Having slyly attempted to turn our unfortunate reader's mind upside down and inside out, let us examine the practical world for a while...

> A practical man is a man who has the instinct for this economy of time and means, and who obtains it all the more easily as his goal is clearer and better localized: an external object.
> [...] Dance is quite the opposite. [...] there is, in itself, no reason, no tendency specific to completion. A formula for pure dance must not contain anything that would indicate that it will have an end.

> *Philosophie de la Danse* - P 31

The size of the mind of the practical man is determined by that of the external object that he covets, with of course the necessary excess margin of mind to deal with the difficulties and imponderables of the path which separates him from his goal, but no more. In one way or another, his attention, his sense of observation, the course of his thoughts, his imagination even, find themselves reduced, restricted by the quest he is pursuing.

Once he has achieved his goal, the tension that animated him collapses and he is suddenly confronted with a strange quality of emptiness. From the more or less admirable or formidable man of action that he was – or thought he wa – until then, he now finds himself reduced to the rank of upstart. Achieving his goal not only completes his quest, but for a while it also completes the man. Even if he had set himself the goal of becoming emperor, having achieved his goal, he is well advanced. Invested with all the powers, he must test them as soon as possible, and therefore immediately imagine something to desire, something arbitrary preferably, in order to demonstrate his recovered freedom after the achieving of his goal. *Anything* can do the trick, but when summoned to appear, this anything refuses to come to fruition. The arbitrary, when summoned to manifest itself, refuses to do so, and even within the emperor's mind, the spirit persists in blowing only when and where it wants.

Thus, another dancer, Salome, having admirably danced at Herod's banquet, is offered by the dazzled king "whatever she wants, even if it is half of his kingdom". Barely out of her choreographic reverie, the young girl wants nothing, except probably to continue or resume her dance. She then turns to her mother Herodias and asks, "*What should I want?*'. A question that the newly hatched emperor, certainly does not have the possibility of publicly asking his mother.

The dancer, the one Valéry tells us about, just like the Salomé in the tale, has no external goal. But truth be told, *she has no inner goal either.* Her movements bring out space, manifest it as space from the heart of this *vertical poetic moment* that Gaston Bachelard speaks of. And, because it is vertical, this moment has no – and does not want any – beginning nor end. Which in no way means that it is "out of time". It is still in time, but this time has become *vertical.* It no longer fits into the usual – realistic – sequence of events. It no longer passes, it hatches, it develops into a different dimension of time. It is a kind of time that is self-created and self-maintaining, a sort of gliding flight of time from which all wings beats have disappeared. A time without noise and where, alone, silently flows, the flow from Hugo's *Mouth of Shadow.*
"*O Time suspend your flight*" says Lamartine from the edge of a lake which he remembers, and, as an initiate of poetic slowness, he adds: "*I say to this night: Be slower*". And here we find this addiction to the time of intellectual creativity that we spoke about above.

But for not having a goal, the dancer nonetheless has an interior life, and even an intense interior life with a particularly tight texture, precisely *because she has no goal...*

> And so, allow me some bold expression, could we not consider it, and I have already made you sense it, as a way of interior life, by now giving, to this term of psychology, a new meaning where the physiology dominates?

Philosophie de la danse - P 32

Although Paul Valéry has most of the time been considered "a man of the intellect", we see from this remark that – unlike religious people and philosophers – he perceives the fundamental unity of body and spirit and that he perceives it in its reality and its effectiveness, that is to say in its *dynamics* since he designates this unity "as an enclosure of resonances".

Reference is here made to what is called, in current sciences, *somesthesia*, that is to say the subset of the nervous system which allows the dynamic perception of the body, based on information developed by several tens of millions sensors, of around ten different types, distributed throughout the entire body. With regard to dance, it is more precisely two subsets of the somesthesia associated with the internal perception of movements, which are *proprioception* and *kinesthesia*. In the case of activities that are both physical and intellectual such as dance, music, sports, but also many others, internal perceptions and external perceptions are dynamically coupled at all times to enable execution of any action and especially any corrections to be made to the progress of movements. This is why Valéry is astonishingly acute when he talks about *resonance*, a term that is ultimately more exact and clearer than the rather flat usual term of *coupling*.

One more step in this direction and we would find ourselves faced with this Buddhist conception of consciousness as explained in certain texts by the biologist Francisco Varela, that is to say, *an additional sense to the other senses* and which would ultimately be nothing other than the (dynamic!) *perception of the perceiving activity of the other senses*. A *perception of perception* in short. That is to say something very close to the type of resonance that Valéry talks about above.

Yet, the fact remains that *consciousness is not thought*. And besides, the opposite is no less true. Consciousness – quite naturally according to what has just been said – is essentially *perception*. Thought, on the other hand, is about *action*. Thought combines, manipulates, plays and replays with *models* that it constantly constructs and adapts, and it wanders in *simulations* which, for the most part, *are not conscious*. This is what dreams demonstrate – as soon as we stop looking for meaning in them and focus first on the way they present themselves. The simulations that dreams offer us are so perfect, so exact – since not contradicted by perceptions, external or internal – that we believe we are *there*. And sometimes, the impressions are so vivid and so violent that we would prefer not to believe them.

However, an enigma remains, about which Valéry says nothing, but which the mathematician Henri Poincaré in chapter 3 entitled *The Mathematical Invention* of his book *Science and Method* attempts to confront: *consciousness sorts.*

At a given moment, consciousness does not simultaneously present to us all the information that our senses develop and offer us. According to Poincaré, the same is true of conscious thought, which selects what is appropriate within the moires and iridescence of the underlying unconscious thinking activity. Valéry, as a good disciple of Mallarmé, states that "Every thought emits a throw of the Dice" and that hence thought is based on chance, both in terms of its sources and in its movement. Poincaré tries to get out of this situation by positing that the principle of selection of what ultimately reaches consciousness in mathematics is beauty – which does not resolve much, unless taking the risk of wandering to define what beauty consists of, which is hardly less thorny. But, experienced in taking into account the immensity of the combinatorics and of the chances involved, Poincaré is well aware that he is not finished with the problem.

It does not seem, moreover, that Surrealism really raised the question of the dynamics of thought. It was more often content with collecting the marvels, the *results* of what it ended up calling *automatism*, rather than to grasp and understand the underlying movements which gave rise to marvels. But in fact, *the true functioning of thought* was not, and can in no way be an automatism, because life is not automatic and neither is thought, may it be conscious or unconscious.
We can here foresee the inaugural limits of the field of surrealist investigation from its very original definition: "The *expression* of the real functioning of thought". Not the passionate and exciting *investigation* of the real functioning of thought, of its dynamics, but only its *expression*. As for the dynamics of the intellect, a ready-made solution was already there, available. Psychoanalysis, which claimed to provide an explanation for everything, and even for the rest, appeared to be sufficient as regarded providing an understanding of the dynamics of the mind, nipping in the bud, so to speak, everything that could have led further and deeper.

But let's return to the *dance model* proposed by Valéry… How are the dancer's movements selected? Of course, the dancer presents to us, in part, what she knows how to do: the movements that she has learned and that she possibly makes according to the threads of a given tradition. But every movement contains an element of risk, and therefore of irremediable improvisation. And the same goes for any interpretation. An actor does not play the same piece every night, nor does a musician play the same piece every time.

But, following the example of Valéry, we must here leave this question open for lack of being able to elucidate what should be called, the mystery, or even the miracle of any gesture.

> It is much simpler to construct a universe than to explain how a man stands on his feet. Ask Aristotle, Descartes, Leibniz and a some others.
>
> *Philosophie de la danse* - P 19

Valéry generalizes in another, very important, direction and indicates that proprioception is also the basis of learning, education and development and is therefore involved in all the arts.

> I tried to communicate to you a fairly abstract idea of Dance, and to represent it to you above all as an action which is deduced, then emerges from ordinary and useful action, and finally opposes it. But this very general point of view (and this is why I adopted it today), leads us to embrace much more than Dance itself. Any action which does not tend towards the useful, and which, on the other hand, is capable of education, improvement, development, is linked to this simplified type of Dance, and, consequently, all the arts can be considered as particular cases of this general idea, since all arts, by definition, include a part of action, the action which produces the work, or which manifests it. […]
>
> *Philosophie de la danse* - P33-34

And he immediately extends what he has just established regarding the arts, to poetry itself.

> To begin to say verses is to enter into a verbal dance.
>
> *Philosophie de la danse* - P34

And even the means and techniques of poetry are considered as dance figures.

What is a metaphor, if not a sort of pirouette of the idea with which
we bring together the various images or the various names? And what
are all these figures that we use, all these means, like rhymes,
inversions, antitheses, if they are not uses of all the possibilities of
language, which detach us from the practical world to form us, too,
our particular universe, privileged place of spiritual dance?

Philosophie de la danse - P41

Which therefore leads him to a conception of *poetry as dance...*

But he goes much further and identifies the contours of *an aesthetics of
the creative process*, an aesthetics of *movement*, quite the opposite of the
traditional aesthetics of the *result.* Between the creative activity, that is to
say the creative process itself, and the artworks, the results created, and
possibly marketable, Valéry immediately made – as much as it was
possible for him – the same choice that he had identified with Leonardo
da Vinci in his *Introduction to the Method of Leonardo da Vinci*; Vinci,
who often preferred the movement of his thought to the completion of his
works, which he happened to finish – and sometimes not.

[...] all the arts are very varied forms of action and are analyzed in
terms of action. [...] you can then conceive of the creation of a work
of art, a work of painting and sculpture, as a work of art itself. The
material object which is shaped under the fingers of the artist being
then nothing more than the pretext, the stage accessory, the subject of
the ballet.
This view seems bold to you, I imagine? But remember that, for many
a great artist, a work is never finished; what they believe to be their
desire for perfection is perhaps only a form of this interior life made
up of energy and sensitivity in reciprocal exchange and as if
reversible.

Philosophie de la danse - P 38

Considering the completed work of art as the simple pretext for a much
fundamental movement in the creative process... That is likely to
dynamite the entire tradition, the entire social structure underlying the
Art Market. Because the process of intellectual creation is as elusive as
the smallest moments of life. You can record a dance performance at
your leisure, but that does not give you access to the inner life of the
dancer who gave birth to it. *We only ever record ashes,* and these ashes
are not fire. We believe we can capture the prey, when we do not catch
even a shadow of it.

The same is true in the arts. The work of art, whatever its price ultimately may be, in no way gives access to years of chance and reflection, to meandering thoughts – and where applicable even laziness – or, on the contrary, to instantaneous flashes and to orgies of immediacy, which ultimately led to what is not even a trace, to what is ultimately *always* a poor result.

And this is why all exhibitions are in vain. An ideology – which is in fact only a variant of censorship – continues to suggest to the public that the essential is in the artwork, supposed to be sufficient in itself. The original artwork of course, in no case a vulgar copy. But the original and the copy are equal and are in truth one and the same thing... A manifestation of nothingness.
Transposed into a more ordinary domain, this ideology supposes considering that the merchandise in the shop window would have an autonomous existence, and that the moments – or entire lives – of work of the human beings who built it would be considered null and void. It is clear what interests such a vision serves, even if its followers claim, on occasion, to be proud anarchists.
Irremediably, real life is elsewhere and it cannot be sold.

The fact remains that in this low – very low – world the artist must still, unfortunately, earn his living, and that in this game, fame is worth what salary is worth. This is what Paul Valéry was more deeply aware of throughout his life than many others.
Because it is to understand nothing that not to take into account the fundamental duplicity of Valéry's daily life and the relationships between his two lives, the morning one, the life of the (unpublished) *Cahiers*, with higher priority in all respects, where he is involves himself, with passion, to the highest exercise of intelligence on the one hand, and that of commissioned works and worldly affairs where he allows himself to be stupid – *as he says* – on the other hand. It is easy – and reasonable – to draw the conclusion that deep down, he only accepts the aesthetics of the result as a way of earning his living, that is to say, as a concession to utility. Yet he only does it out of financial necessity, because he has sometimes been so poor as to have to knowingly produce false manuscripts of his works because they sold better and more expensively than his published works themselves.

But let's leave all this monkey business there because Valéry's thinking leads us to conclusions of a much broader scope.

> I wanted to show you how this art, far from being a futile entertainment, far from being a specialty that is limited to the production of a few shows, to the amusement of the eyes that consider it or the bodies that are doing it, is quite simply a general poetry of the action of living beings.

Philosophie de la danse - P 40

Because yes, reader, you read correctly: what is at stake in this text – timidly and as if surreptitiously – is *a general poetry of the action of living beings*. And this was indeed the meaning of this almost innocuous remark where he identified at the very heart of dance, something as "a way of inner life, by now giving to this psychological term a new meaning where *physiology* dominates?".

As soon as we stop separating the mind from the body, dance and thought appear for what they are: one and the same thing. That is to say *a general poetry...*

Valéry – and it seems that, in this, he has until now remained unique – here considers the dynamics of the arts and thought as the fundamental activity, not of a humanity foreign to nature – and as if fallen from the sky – but of *the entire living kingdom.*

Danser – Penser

Danser – Penser

> *J'ai tendu des cordes de clocher à clocher ; des guirlandes*
> *de fenêtre à fenêtre ; des chaînes d'or d'étoile à étoile, et je*
> *danse.*
>
> Arthur Rimbaud

Le prétexte du texte qui suit est une conférence de Paul Valéry
prononcée le 5 mars 1936 à l'*Université des Annales* et parue dans
Conferencia en novembre 1936. Le texte utilisé ici est celui de la version
publiée par les *éditions Allia* en 2023 sous le titre *Philosophie de la
danse*.

On ne peut qu'espérer que puissent s'appliquer ici les quelques mots
d'introduction de Valéry :

> « Il faut vous résigner à entendre quelques propositions que va,
> devant vous, risquer sur la Danse un homme qui ne danse pas. Vous
> attendrez un peu le moment de la merveille, et vous vous direz que je
> ne suis pas moins impatient que vous d'en être ravi.
> J'entre tout de suite dans mes idées, et je vous dis sans autre
> préparation que la Danse, à mon sens, ne se borne pas à être un
> exercice, un divertissement, un art ornemental, un jeu de société
> quelquefois ; elle est chose sérieuse et, par certains aspects, chose très
> vénérable. »

À l'instar de Valéry, entrons tout de suite dans les idées !

> Les fourmis ne perdent pas une minute. L'araignée guette et ne
> s'amuse pas sur sa toile. Mais l'homme?
> L'homme est cet animal singulier qui se regarde vivre, qui se donne
> une valeur, et qui place toute cette valeur qu'il lui plaît de se donner
> dans l'importance qu'il attache à des perceptions inutiles et à des actes
> sans conséquence physique vitale.
>
> Paul Valéry – *Philosophie de la danse* – P16

Valéry suppose – invente – que les animaux seraient perpétuellement
affairés à leur survie... On en disait de même des hommes de la

préhistoire, avant que le livre *Âge de Pierre, Âge d'Abondance* de Marshall Sahlins ne vienne ramener les économistes à la raison. Quelques observations ethnographiques auraient pu y suffire si les économistes avaient été capables de se soucier d'observer avant de pontifier sur des sujets qu'ils ne connaissaient nullement. Au reste, peu émus par les faits, on voit d'ailleurs un peu partout qu'ils persévèrent…

Pour ce qui concerne les fourmis, on sait désormais ce qu'il en est, et que La Fontaine ne pouvait guère savoir : les fourmis donnent certes l'impression d'être toujours au travail, mais ce n'est qu'une impression. Elles se promènent et errent beaucoup, et ne sont pas si travailleuses que ça.

L'homme n'est donc nullement cet artisan de l'inutile, cette exception du monde vivant que Valéry croit s'élever par là au-delà de la condition des autres animaux. Obsédés par la prétendue *sélection naturelle* – par quoi la beaucoup n'ont ordinairement rien d'autre en vue qu'une représentation fantasmagorique de la concurrence capitaliste – la plupart des gens, scientifiques inclus, semblent avoir oublié que pour qu'il puisse y avoir sélection naturelle, il faut bien qu'il y ait eu préalablement *création naturelle,* faute de quoi il y a bien longtemps que la sélection aurait cessé, faute de caractéristiques à sélectionner.

> « On nous parle sans cesse de Dar-win, mais on ne nous dit jamais rien de Dar-lose » s'amusait un ami…

En réalité, les capacités créatives du vivant excèdent de fort loin l'utile, et c'est heureux. Car l'utile n'est identifiable qu'en fonction des circonstances, soit présentes, soit prévisibles à court terme. Mais à plus long terme, à l'échelle de quelques centaines de milliers ou de quelques millions d'années, les circonstances excèdent très vite et de beaucoup les capacités humaines de prévision et d'anticipation… Pour autant, comme chacun peut le constater, même sur des millions d'années, les circonstances n'excèdent aucunement, les capacités créatives du vivant, *pris en tant que système global,* c'est à dire au delà du cas particulier de chaque espèce. Car la vie perdure depuis environ 3,5 milliards d'années, ordre de grandeur de durée qui se trouve, lui aussi, très au-delà des capacités d'imagination des êtres humains.

La vie, pas plus que les hommes eux-mêmes d'ailleurs – quoiqu'ils en prétendent – ne sait le moins du monde où elle va. Elle ne se tire d'affaire que par une créativité effrénée dont la plus grande part a statistiquement toutes les chances de ne servir à rien, et dont seule une infime partie pourra s'avérer utile, à l'occasion, pour d'éventuelles adaptations. Et donc, si l'homme, à l'instar de tout le reste du vivant, est en effet un artisan de l'inutile, cela, comme on vient de le voir, ne disqualifie en rien pour autant l'inutile, au contraire.

> [...] cette pensée qui nous édifie, à nos propres yeux, au-dessus de notre condition sensible est exactement la pensée qui ne sert à rien. [...] Nos pensées les plus profondes sont les plus indifférentes à notre conservation et, en quelque sorte, futiles par rapport à elles.

> *Philosophie de la danse* - P17

Ah ? « indifférentes à notre conservation » ? De quel point de vue ? Vis à vis de quelles échelles de temps ? Et quant à notre conservation, s'agit-il ici de la conservation des individus ou de celle de l'espèce ?

Toute pensée utilitariste est nécessairement une pensée du court terme, une pensée à courte vue puisque le long et le très long terme sont inimaginables, c'est à dire hors d'atteinte de toute pensée. Dès lors, « La pensée qui ne sert à rien », loin de n'être qu'un un monstrueux gaspillage – ce qu'elle est évidemment *aussi* – constitue en fait, quoique infinitésimalement peut-être d'un point de vue statistique, notre seule espérance de survie à long terme en ce qu'elle tente de se porter au-delà de l'imaginable même. Cette errance, ce risque proprement insensé, cette excursion du vivant hors de l'immédiatement utile, bref, ce luxe inouï, est en fait au cœur de cette étrange volonté de vivre qui nous porte, nous et la vie toute entière.

Bien entendu, ce qui, avec un peu de recul et de distance, au travers la diversité des circonstances et des espèces nous apparaît comme une sorte *d'orgie de créativité* du vivant, ne vaut que pour autant que cela ne s'oppose pas à la diversité des caractéristiques accumulées à l'intérieur de chaque individu comme à l'intérieur de chaque espèce, ni à l'accumulation de la diversité des espèces destinée à faire face à la diversité des circonstances, ni bien entendu à cette règle fondamentale du jeu qui est la capacité de se reproduire.

Philosophie de la danse - P17

Valéry entrevoit – *presque* – la nécessité biologique de l'inutile lorsqu'il considère *la curiosité*, faculté bien plus qu'humaine, dont il sait fort bien que les animaux ne sont de toute évidence nullement dépourvus. Comme il sait bien aussi que toute curiosité, qu'elle soit animale ou humaine, est par définition même de la curiosité, *en excès*, c'est à dire *plus avide qu'il n'est nécessaire*. Et c'est même à cela qu'on reconnaît la curiosité. Mais au lieu de comprendre la curiosité humaine comme le prolongement – sans doute hypertrophié – d'une curiosité animale sous-jacente préalable, d'une curiosité animale *issue de l'évolution biologique* et dont *émerge* la curiosité humaine, sans cela incompréhensible et comme « tombée du ciel », Valéry se concentre (et à juste titre !) sur l'inutilité foncière, radicale, des civilisations elles-mêmes et de leurs produits, « *dont on pouvait facilement se passer* ».

Pourquoi se livre-t-on avec tant d'ardeur à la production d'objets de formes et d'actions dont on pouvait facilement se passer ? C'est en vertu d'un autre aspect sur lequel Valéry revient souvent – et sur lequel il faudra bien, en effet, revenir – qui est le caractère proprement *addictif* des processus de la créativité intellectuelle.

Philosophie de la danse - P 19

Si l'on convient – avec quelque répugnance et très temporairement – d'accepter la séparation qu'établit Valéry entre le producteur et le consommateur de créativité intellectuelle (dans son *Cours de Poétique* au Collège de France), alors il faut considérer l'addiction provoquée par la création intellectuelle selon ces deux versants : celui de la production et celui de la consommation. Et dans cette perspective, la danse apparaît, à Valéry comme à nous-mêmes, comme un exemple très pur du processus d'addiction du producteur dont le mouvement échappe à la réalité, c'est à dire à tout réel *convenu*.

> [...] la danseuse est dans un autre monde, qui n'est plus celui qui se peint de nos regards, mais celui qu'elle tisse de ses pas et construit de ses gestes. Mais, dans ce monde-là, il n'y a point de but extérieur aux actes; il n'y a pas d'objet à saisir, à rejoindre ou à repousser ou à fuir, un objet qui termine exactement une action et donne aux mouvements, d'abord, une direction et une coordination extérieures, et ensuite une conclusion nette et certaine.

> *Philosophie de la danse* - P 27-28

Certes le mouvement de la danseuse échappe à tout but extérieur à celui – en actes – du corps et de l'esprit de la danseuse, mais Valéry du même mouvement nous livre un secret que seuls les mathématiciens qui créèrent les nouvelles conceptions de la géométrie vers la fin du XIXe siècle – par exemple Henri Poincaré – auraient pu nous révéler si nous avions eu l'audace de les lire. Un secret qui est que l'espace n'est pas ce continu infini et vide que créa ex-nihilo Newton (et plus généralement le XVIIe siècle) mais qu'il est au contraire défini (construit) par les groupes de transformations (i.e. rotations, translations, etc...) qui y opèrent.

Autrement dit, l'espace n'est pas une donnée en soi, une sorte de décor de théâtre pré-existant au sein duquel viendraient s'inscrire notre vie et notre geste, mais que – à un niveau intuitif du moins – il est au contraire *tissé et construit* par nos actes et par nos gestes. (Voir *Pourquoi l'espace a 3 dimensions* in *Dernières Pensées,* Henri Poincaré 1913, Flammarion 1917). Plus précisément Poincaré montre que notre intuition de l'espace repose essentiellement sur la notion de *mouvement.* Sur la *perception interne* – musculaire – *des mouvements* de notre corps.

Voilà une approche qui fait résonner étrangement le mot de Marx : dans la dynamique de la danse, la différence entre interprétation et transformation s'effondre car l'espace, *invoqué* puis *créé* par le mouvement de la danseuse, se trouve simultanément interprété et transformé – plus exactement, interprété *parce que* transformé par les actes. Cela nous révèle que le sens du mot *interprétation* dans la phrase de Marx ne visait qu'une interprétation *abstraire,* c'est à dire *non-physiquement vécue* – c'est à dire d'une certaine façon comme on le suggérera plus loin*, non-dansée.*

Poincaré explique de l'espace n'est pas cet absolu vide dont parlait Newton, mais qu'il est essentiellement *relatif* :

> Je veux dire par là, non seulement que nous pourrions être transportés dans une autre région de l'espace sans nous en apercevoir (et c'est effectivement ce qui arrive puisque nous ne nous apercevons pas de la translation de la Terre), non seulement que toutes les dimensions des objets pourraient être augmentées dans une même proportion, sans que nous puissions le savoir, pourvu que nos instruments de mesure participent à cet agrandissement ; mais que je veux dire encore que l'espace pourrait être déformé suivant une loi arbitraire, pourvu que nos instruments de mesure soient déformés précisément d'après la même loi

Henri Poincaré, Dernières pensées, P61-62

Et il précise juste après que ce qu'il entend par « loi arbitraire » est *une déformation continue*.

> L'espace, considéré indépendamment de nos instruments de mesure, n'a donc ni propriété métrique, ni propriété projective ; il n'a que des propriétés topologiques. Il est amorphe, c'est à dire qu'il ne diffère pas de celui qu'on en déduirait par une déformation continue quelconque.

Henri Poincaré, Dernières pensées, P62

On sent immédiatement combien cette vision de l'espace conçu comme *essentiellement déformable* est proche de celle l'espace-temps déformable de la *Théorie de la Relativité* – à l'élaboration de laquelle Poincaré participa d'ailleurs largement.

Poincaré nous explique donc qu'il existe quelque chose de sous-jacent à l'espace usuel, quelque chose de plus profond, qui est ce qui permet au mathématicien de *bien raisonner sur des figures mal faites* (*Dernières pensées,* P59-70), qui est ce qu'étudie la discipline des mathématiques qu'on appelle désormais la *Topologie* et qui s'avère être l'étude d'un espace *amorphe*, c'est à dire *sans formes* – puisque déformable à loisir.

Mais alors, revenant à la danseuse de Valéry, la question se pose de la nature du matériau préalable à la création de l'espace que la danseuse tisse et construit de ses pas et de ses gestes. Il ne s'agit évidemment pas d'un espace, puisque l'espace justement, c'est la danseuse qui le crée.

Nous vivons encore, pour la plupart, avec l'idée, finalement plutôt incongrue, d'un espace infini, sans soupçonner ce que cette représentation peut avoir de religieux, c'est à dire de proprement *terroriste*. En témoigne, au revers de ses bondieuseries cette révélation angoissée de Blaise Pascal : « le silence éternel de ces espaces infinis m'effraie... ». A quoi, la pensée du bon Gaston Bachelard répond sans trembler : « Je ne vis pas dans l'infini, parce que dans l'infini, on n'est pas chez soi ». Révélant par là que le rôle, que la fonction, de tous ces infinis n'avait en fait pour raison d'être que de nous chasser de chez nous, *de notre monde*. De faire de nous *des étrangers définitifs*.

Dans la nouvelle géométrie que nous révèlent à la fois les mathématiques et la danse, en revanche, nous sommes indéracinablement chez nous puisque ce sont nos mouvements et nos actes qui tissent et construisent un espace au-delà duquel il ne saurait y avoir qu'un *Apeiron*, dépourvu de *périmètre* (les deux termes ont même racine étymologique), c'est à dire un *indéterminé*, un *indéfini, mais non pas un illimité au sens usuel du mot.*

Bien sûr, pris à la lettre, *illimité* signifie sans limites, mais il s'agit alors d'une absence, d'un *défaut de limite*, qui n'a rien à voir avec un quelconque infini. Si le terrain de mon voisin n'a pas été borné, il est correct de dire qu'il est sans bornes. Mais personne n'en conclura pour autant qu'il est illimité au sens d'infini. Si, en outre, par suite d'un oubli, il ne figure même pas au cadastre alors il est *indéterminé, indéfini*, mais il n'est pas pour autant infini. Si on traduit « rigoureusement », au pied de la lettre, le mot *Apeiron* par *illimité*, au sens usuel qu'il a pris, d'infini, alors réversiblement, j'ai le droit de prétendre que s*i Dieu est infini, c'est qu'il n'est pas tout à fait terminé*, ce qui me vaudra probablement l'ire de la plupart des théologiens.
Autrement dit, *Apeiron* ne signifie ni illimité, ni infini. Un infini qui, d'ailleurs, partout et toujours, ne se révèle jamais comme rien d'autre que la répétition du même.

Et puis, sauf à faire de la culture de l'ignorance une méthode propre à l'exploration des mystères du Réel, il est devenu intellectuellement malhonnête de ne pas tenir compte des trouvailles du mathématicien Georg Cantor selon lesquelles il existe différentes sortes d'infinis, des grands et des petits, que l'on peut en quelque sorte *emboîter* les uns dans les autres… Ainsi l'ensemble des entiers naturels est-il infini à sa manière particulière (dénombrable), mais il peut être inclus – Il *est* généralement inclus – dans l'ensemble des nombres réels qui est lui-aussi infini, mais d'une manière différente et tout à fait singulière puisque l'ensemble des nombres réels compris (par exemple) entre 0 et 1 n'est pas moins infini que l'ensemble de tous les nombres réels pris dans leur totalité, ce qui peut sembler assez vertigineux.

Mais nous ne sommes pourtant pas pour cela au bout de nos vertiges puisque Cantor montre qu'il n'existe pas plus d'éléments dans un espace de dimension N (N entier fini) que de nombres réels compris entre 0 et 1 (ou dans l'ensemble des nombres réels tout entier). Confronté à cette évidence (mathématique) Cantor est si surpris de sa découverte qu'il écrit : « Je le *vois*, mais je ne le *crois* pas ! ».

Ce que les découvertes de Cantor révèlent en l'espèce, c'est que quand on parle d'un espace de dimension N, on ne fait jamais que parler d'une *structuration particulière* d'un ensemble infini d'éléments dont le nombre n'est « pas plus grand » que le nombre d'éléments d'un espace de dimension 1. Mais un espace de dimension 1, tel que, par exemple, l'ensemble des nombre réels, ne correspond lui-même qu'à une *structuration particulière* (celle qui définit les nombres réels) d'un ensemble infini disons, « de grande taille » – de taille supérieure en tous cas à la taille de l'ensemble infini des entiers naturels.

Mais ces différentes structurations sont des *contraintes* (diraient les pataphysiciens), qui viennent *déterminer*, *définir* des formes *dans*, ou bien plutôt, *à partir de*, l'Apeiron, des *formes* qui nous permettent en quelque sorte d'explorer quelques petits bouts de ce qui peut naître de l'Apeiron, des formes sans lesquelles nous ne saurions absolument rien en dire. Car l'Apeiron d'Anaximandre est ce qui n'a ni formes ni qualités déterminées.

En somme la danseuse mathématique procède de la même manière que la danseuse de Valéry, elle fait des gestes (elle élabore des axiomes, des définitions, des démonstrations et des théorèmes), *des gestes de pensée* sans doute, mais des gestes tout de même, et ces gestes tissent et construisent… Non pas l'espace, certes non, mais bien les mathématiques.

Dans la vision d'Anaximandre, c'est l'Apeiron lui-même qui, à tout instant, est l'activité qui génère toutes les formes, minérales, végétales ou animales. Les humains – et leurs créations – n'en étant qu'un cas particulier.

Aussi, plutôt que de suivre les méandres de Heidegger, tout en trahissant en partie – et joyeusement – Anaximandre, on préférera ici interpréter l'Apeiron sous l'aspect chinois du *Tao, comme cet indéterminé d'où émergent toutes les formes,* ou si l'on préfère peut-être sous les atours du *vide quantique,* tout aussi créatif, ou encore comme cette *Bouche d'Ombre* dont parle Victor Hugo dans *Les Contemplations.*

Et c'est en quoi Valéry peut comparer la danse et le rêve, et dire de la danseuse en actes...

> Rien n'existe au-delà du système qu'elle se forme par ses actes, système qui fait songer au système tout contraire et non moins fermé que nous constitue le sommeil, dont la loi tout opposée est l'abolition, l'abstention totale des actes.

Philosophie de la danse - P 29

À quoi se reconnaît une certaine répugnance de Valéry quant au rêve, mot qu'il prend grand soin ici de contourner en se référant au sommeil. Peine perdue toutefois, puisque ni le sommeil ni le rêve ne font montre d'une *abstention totale des actes* et qu'il suffit d'observer les subreptices mouvements qu'ébauchent un chat ou un chien qui rêvent, ou même plus simplement ceux de son prochain endormi, pour saisir ce qui très étrangement manque ici à Valéry, et qui est la compréhension de l'esprit comme *activité simulatrice.*

Car nous savons désormais, et de façon scientifique, que ni les mouvements ni les actes ne sont absents des rêves. Nous savons qu'ils y sont présents, *simulés* et *inhibés*, et qu'il leur arrive parfois de s'échapper dans le réel, hors du sommeil et hors du rêve, hors de cette supposée *abstention totale des actes*, dont parle Valéry.

Toutefois, ce qui semble être au cœur de la remarque de Valéry qui précède en fait, c'est plutôt l'idée d'une *clôture,* d'une dynamique de la danseuse qui se referme sur *le système qu'elle se forme par ses actes.* De sorte que ce que cette clôture désigne, c'est cet Apeiron que constitue l'au-delà de ses mouvements. Un indéterminé et un indéfini qui ne sont *même pas* de l'espace, puisque l'espace est ce que *tissent* et *construisent* à tout instant les actes de la danseuse et qu'ils n'ont pas encore *déterminé* et *défini* cet Apeiron qui apparaît ainsi comme ce qu'il est : *une absence d'espace.*

Mais ce *système* que la danseuse se forme, nous conduit à un autre Apeiron. Car il faut bien que ce système que se forme la danseuse soit lui-même issu d'un autre indéterminé, d'un autre indéfini, mais *interne cette fois*, dont les moires s'agitent et s'évanouissent à tout instant au sein de la danseuse et qui constitue la source même de ses actes. De sorte que si, armés du *Coup de Dés* de Mallarmé, nous admettons que « toute pensée émet un coup de dés », alors il nous faut admettre qu'il en va de même des actes de la danseuse qui, pas moins que ne le font nos pensées, sourdent et se détachent sur un fond de *hasard.* De sorte qu'à l'Apeiron *externe* il nous faut ajouter un autre Apeiron, un autre indéterminé, un autre indéfini, mais *interne.*
Et, au point où nous en sommes, par le truchement mental, par la magie, d'une Bouteille de Klein – objet bien connu dont l'intérieur est aussi l'extérieur – nous pouvons en venir à soupçonner qu'en cette matière, l'Apeiron *externe* et l'Apeiron *interne* ne font qu'un.

Après avoir sournoisement tenté de mettre l'esprit de notre infortuné lecteur sens dessus dessous, examinons ce qu'il en est du monde pratique.

> Un homme pratique est un homme qui a l'instinct de cette économie de temps et de moyens, et qui l'obtient d'autant plus aisément que son but est plus net et mieux localisé: un objet extérieur. [...] La danse, c'est tout le contraire. [...] il n'y a, en elle-même, aucune raison, aucune tendance propre à l'achèvement. Une formule de la danse pure ne doit rien contenir qui fasse prévoir qu'elle ait un terme.
>
> *Philosophie de la danse* - P 31

La taille de l'esprit de l'homme pratique est déterminée par celle de l'objet *extérieur* qu'il convoite, avec bien sûr ce qu'il faut de marge excédentaire d'esprit pour parer aux difficultés et aux impondérables du chemin qui le sépare de son but, *mais pas plus.* D'une manière ou d'une autre, son attention, son sens de l'observation, le cours de ses pensées, son imagination même, se trouvent réduits, restreints par la quête qu'il poursuit.

Une fois arrivé à ses fins, la tension qui l'animait s'effondre et le voilà soudain confronté à une étrange qualité de vide. De l'homme d'action plus ou moins admirable ou redoutable qu'il était – ou se vivait – jusque là, il se trouve désormais réduit au rang de *parvenu*. L'atteinte du but n'achève pas seulement la quête, pour un temps elle achève l'homme aussi. Quand bien même se serait-il donné pour but de devenir empereur, ayant atteint son but, le voilà bien avancé. Investi de tous les pouvoirs, il lui faut en faire l'essai dans les meilleurs délais, et donc imaginer sur le champ quelque chose à désirer, quelque chose d'arbitraire de préférence, de sorte de faire montre de sa liberté retrouvée après l'atteinte de son but. *N'importe quoi* peut faire l'affaire, mais sommé d'apparaître ce *n'importe quoi* refuse de venir à point. L'arbitraire, sommé se se manifester, s'y refuse et chez l'empereur même, l'esprit persiste à ne souffler que quand et où il veut.

Ainsi une autre danseuse, Salomé, ayant admirablement dansé au banquet d'Hérode, se voit-elle offrir par le roi ébloui « ce qu'elle voudra, fût-ce la moitié de son royaume ». À peine sortie de sa rêverie chorégraphique, la jeune fille ne veut rien, sauf, probablement , continuer ou reprendre sa danse. Elle se tourne alors vers sa mère Hérodiade et demande : « *Que faut-il vouloir ?* ». Une question que l'empereur, tout frais éclos, n'a certes pas la possibilité protocolaire de poser publiquement à sa maman.

La danseuse, celle dont nous entretient Valéry, tout comme la Salomé du conte, n'a pas de but extérieur. Mais à vrai dire, elle n'a pas de but intérieur non plus. Ses mouvements font surgir l'espace, le manifestent comme espace depuis le cœur de cet instant poétique vertical dont parle Gaston Bachelard. Et, parce qu'il est vertical, cet instant n'a – ni ne veut – aucun commencement ni aucune fin. Ce qui ne signifie nullement qu'il soit pour autant « hors du temps ». Il est toujours dans le temps, mais ce temps est devenu *vertical.* Il ne s'insère plus dans la séquence usuelle – réaliste – des événements. Il ne passe plus, il éclot. C'est un temps qui s'auto-crée et qui s'auto-entretien, une sorte de vol plané du temps d'où tous battements d'ailes ont disparu. Un temps sans bruit et où seul, silencieusement coule le flux de la *bouche d'ombre* de Hugo.
« *O Temps suspends ton vol* » dit Lamartine du bord d'un *Lac* dont il se remémore, et en initié des lenteurs poétiques, il ajoute : « *Je dis à cette*

nuit : Sois plus lente ». Et on retrouve ici cette addiction au temps de la créativité intellectuelle dont nous parlions plus haut.

Mais pour ne pas avoir de but, la danseuse n'en a pas moins une vie intérieure, et même une vie intérieure intense et d'une texture particulièrement serrée, *justement parce qu'elle n'a pas de but...*

> Et donc, permettez-moi quelque expression hardie, ne pourrait-on la considérer, et je vous l'ai déjà fait pressentir, comme une manière de vie intérieure, en donnant à présent, à ce terme de psychologie, un sens nouveau où la physiologie domine?
> Vie intérieure, mais celle-ci toute construite de sensations de durée et de sensations d'énergie qui se répondent, et forment comme une enceinte de résonances.

Philosophie de la danse - P 32

Bien que Paul Valéry ait la plupart du temps été considéré comme « un homme de l'intellect», on voit par cette remarque que – contrairement aux religieux et aux philosophes – il perçoit l'unité fondamentale du corps et de l'esprit et qu'il la perçoit dans sa réalité et son effectivité, c'est à dire dans sa *dynamique* puisqu'il désigne cette unité « comme une enceinte de résonances » .

Il est fait ici référence à ce qui s'appelle, dans les sciences actuelles, la *somesthésie*, c'est à dire le sous-ensemble du système nerveux qui permet la perception dynamique du corps, à partir des informations élaborées par plusieurs dizaines de millions de capteurs, d'une dizaine de types différents, distribués dans le corps tout entier.

Pour ce qui concerne la danse, il s'agit plus précisément de deux sous-ensembles de la somesthésie associés à la perception *interne* des mouvements, et qui sont la *proprioception* et la *kinesthésie*. Dans le cas des activités qui sont à la fois physiques et intellectuelles comme par exemple la danse, la musique, les sports, mais aussi beaucoup d'autres, les perceptions internes et les perceptions externes sont dynamiquement couplées *à tout instant* pour permettre l'exécution de toute action et surtout les corrections éventuelles à apporter au déroulement des mouvements. C'est en quoi Valéry est d'une acuité étonnante lorsqu'il parle de *résonance*, terme finalement plus exact et plus net que le terme usuel assez plat de *couplage*.

Un pas de plus dans cette direction et on se retrouverait face à cette conception bouddhiste de la conscience explicitée dans certains textes du biologiste Francisco Varela comme un sens additionnel aux autres sens et qui ne serait finalement rien d'autre que la perception (dynamique!) de l'activité perceptrice des autres sens. *Une perception de la perception* en somme. C'est-à-dire quelque chose de très proche du type de résonance dont Valéry parle ci-dessus.

Il reste que la conscience n'est pas la pensée. Et d'ailleurs, l'inverse n'est pas moins vrai. La conscience – assez naturellement selon ce qui vient d'être dit – est essentiellement *perception*. La pensée en revanche, est de l'ordre de *l'action*. La pensée combine, manipule, joue et re-joue avec des *modèles* qu'elle construit et adapte en permanence et elle erre en des *simulations* qui, pour une immense part ne sont pas conscientes. C'est ce dont témoignent les rêves – dès que l'on cesse de leur chercher un sens pour s'intéresser d'abord à la manière dont ils se présentent. Les *simulations* que nous offrent les rêves sont si parfaites, si exactes – non contredites par les perceptions, externes ni internes – *qu'on s'y croirait*. Et parfois, les impressions sont si vives et si violentes, qu'on préférerait ne pas s'y croire.

Il demeure cependant une énigme, dont Valéry ne dit rien, mais que Henri Poincaré dans le chapitre 3 intitulé *L'invention Mathématique* de son livre *Science et Méthode* tente d'affronter : *la conscience trie*.
À un instant donné, la conscience ne nous présente pas en même temps toutes les informations qu'élaborent et nous offrent tous nos sens. Il en va de même selon Poincaré de la pensée inconsciente qui sélectionne *ce qui convient* au sein du fourmillement ou peut-être plutôt des *moires* et des *irisations* des pensées inconscientes sous-jacentes.

Valéry, en bon disciple de Mallarmé pose que « Toute pensée émet un coup de Dés » et que la pensée repose sur le *hasard*, tant quant à ses sources que dans son mouvement. Poincaré tente de se tirer d'affaire en posant que le principe de sélection de ce qui finalement parvient à la conscience en mathématique, c'est la *beauté* – ce qui ne résout pas grand-chose, sauf à définir en quoi consiste la beauté, ce qui n'est guère moins épineux. Mais, rompu à la prise en compte de l'immensité des combinatoires et des hasards mis en jeu, Poincaré est bien conscient qu'il n'en a pas fini avec le problème.

Il ne semble pas d'ailleurs que le Surréalisme se soit vraiment posé la question de la dynamique de la pensée. Il s'est plus souvent contenté de cueillir les merveilles, les *résultats* de ce qu'il a appelé *l'automatisme*, plutôt que de saisir et de comprendre les mouvements sous-jacents qui les faisaient naître. Il ne s'agissait et il ne peut en aucun cas s'agir d'un automatisme, car la vie n'est pas automatique et la pensée, consciente comme inconsciente, ne l'est pas non plus. On peut augurer des limites inaugurales du champ d'investigation surréaliste depuis sa définition originelle même : « *L'expression* du fonctionnement réel de la pensée ». Non pas *l'investigation* passionnée et passionnante du fonctionnement réel de la pensée, de sa dynamique, mais seulement son *expression*. Quant à la dynamique de l'intellect, on tenait une solution, donc *la* solution, toute faite. La psychanalyse, qui prétendait fournir une explication à tout et même au reste, a semblé suffire pourvoir à la compréhension de la dynamique de l'esprit, tuant pour ainsi dire dans l'œuf tout ce qui aurait pu mener plus loin et plus profond.

Mais revenons au modèle de la danse proposé par Valéry… Comment sont sélectionnés les mouvements de la danseuse ? Bien sûr, la danseuse nous présente *pour une part*, ce qu'elle sait faire : les mouvements qu'elle a appris et qu'elle enchaîne possiblement selon les fils d'une tradition donnée. Mais tout mouvement contient une part de risque, et donc *d'improvisation* irrémédiable. Et il en va de même de toute interprétation. Un acteur ne joue pas la même pièce tous les soirs et un musicien ne joue pas non plus chaque fois le même morceau.

Mais, à l'exemple de Valéry, il nous faut ici laisser ouverte cette question, faute de pouvoir élucider ce qu'il faut bien appeler le mystère ou même le miracle de tout geste.

> Il est beaucoup plus simple de construire un univers que d'expliquer comment un homme tient sur ses pieds. Demandez à Aristote, à Descartes, à Leibniz et à quelques autres.

Philosophie de la danse - P 19

Valéry généralise dans une autre direction, très importante, et indique que la proprioception est aussi à la base de l'apprentissage, de l'éducation et du développement et se trouve donc mise en jeu dans tous les arts.

J'ai essayé de vous communiquer une idée assez abstraite de la Danse,
et de vous la représenter surtout comme une action qui se déduit, puis
se dégage de l'action ordinaire et utile, et finalement s'y oppose. Mais
ce point de vue d'une très grande généralité (et c'est pourquoi je l'ai
adopté aujourd'hui), conduit à embrasser beaucoup plus que la danse
proprement dite. Toute action qui ne tend pas à l'utile, et qui, d'autre
part, est susceptible d'éducation, de perfectionnement, de
développement, se rattache à ce type simplifié de la danse, et, par
conséquent, tous les arts peuvent être considérés comme des cas
particuliers de cette idée générale, puisque tous les arts, par
définition, comportent une partie d'action, l'action qui produit l'œuvre,
ou bien qui la manifeste. [...]

Philosophie de la danse - P33-34

Et il étend aussitôt ce qu'il a établi quant aux arts à la poésie elle-même.

Commencer de dire des vers, c'est entrer dans une danse verbale.

Philosophie de la danse - P34

Et jusqu'à ses moyens et à ses techniques envisagées à l'instar des
figures de danse.

Qu'est-ce qu'une métaphore, si ce n'est une sorte de pirouette de l'idée
dont on rapproche les diverses images ou les divers noms? Et que
sont toutes ces figures dont nous usons, tous ces moyens, comme les
rimes, les inversions, les antithèses, si ce ne sont des usages de toutes
les possibilités du langage, qui nous détachent du monde pratique
pour nous former, nous aussi, notre univers particulier, lieu privilégié
de la danse spirituelle?

Philosophie de la danse - P41

Ce qui le conduit donc à une conception de la poésie comme danse...

Mais il va beaucoup plus loin et identifie les contours *d'une esthétique
du processus créatif*, d'une esthétique du mouvement, tout à l'opposé
d'une esthétique du résultat. Entre l'activité créatrice, c'est à dire le
processus de création lui-même, et les œuvres, les *résultats* créés et
éventuellement monnayables, Valéry a d'emblée fait – autant qu'il lui
était possible – le même choix qu'il avait identifié chez Léonard de Vinci
dans son *Introduction à la Méthode de Léonard de Vinci*. Vinci, qui

souvent préférait le mouvement de sa pensée à l'achèvement ses propres
œuvres, qu'il lui est certes arrivé de terminer – et quelque fois pas.

> [...] tous les arts sont des formes très variées de l'action et s'analysent
> en termes d'action. [...] vous pouvez alors concevoir la réalisation
> d'une œuvre d'art, une œuvre de peinture et de sculpture, comme une
> œuvre d'art elle-même, dont l'objet matériel qui se façonne sous les
> doigts de l'artiste n'est plus que le prétexte, l'accessoire de scène, le
> sujet du ballet.
> Cette vue vous paraît hardie, j'imagine? Mais songez que, pour maint
> grand artiste, une œuvre n'est jamais achevée; ce qu'ils croient être
> leur désir de perfection n'est peut-être qu'une forme de cette vie
> intérieure toute faite d'énergie et de sensibilité en échange réciproque
> et comme réversible,

Philosophie de la danse - P 38

Considérer l'œuvre d'art achevée comme le simple prétexte d'un
mouvement beaucoup fondamental, celui du processus de création, voilà
qui est de nature à dynamiter toute la tradition, toute la structure sociale
sous-jacente au Marché de l'Art. Car le processus de la création
intellectuelle est aussi insaisissable que le moindre des instants de vie.
On peut enregistrer à loisir un spectacle de danse, mais cela ne donne pas
pour autant accès à cette vie intérieure de la danseuse qui lui a donné
naissance. On n'enregistre jamais que des cendres, et ces cendres ne sont
pas le feu. On croit pouvoir capturer la proie, quant on n'en saisit pas
même une ombre.

Il en va de même dans le domaine des arts. L'œuvre d'art, quel qu'en soit
finalement le prix, ne donne en aucun cas accès aux années de hasards et
de réflexions, aux méandres de pensée – et le cas échéant de paresse
même – ou au contraire de fulgurances instantanées et d'orgies
d'immédiateté qui ont finalement conduit à ce qui n'est pas même trace,
à ce qui n'est jamais au fond qu'un toujours piètre *résultat*.
Et c'est en quoi toutes les expositions sont vaines. Une idéologie – qui
n'est à vrai dire qu'une variante de censure – continue de suggérer au
public que l'essentiel serait dans l'œuvre, supposée se suffire à elle-
même. L'œuvre originale bien entendu, en aucun cas dans une vulgaire
copie. Mais l'original et la copie se valent et ne sont au vrai qu'une seule
et même chose... Une manifestation du néant.
Transposée dans un domaine plus ordinaire, cette idéologie suppose de
considérer que la marchandise dans la vitrine aurait une existence

38

autonome, et que les instants – ou les vies entières – de travail des êtres humains qui l'ont construite seraient à tenir pour nuls et non advenus. On voit assez quels intérêts sert une pareille vision, quand bien même ses sectateurs prétendraient, à l'occasion, être de farouches anarchistes. Irrémédiablement, la vraie vie est ailleurs et elle n'est pas vendable.

Il n'empêche qu'en ce bas – très bas – monde l'artiste doit encore, hélas, gagner sa vie, et qu'à ce jeu, la célébrité vaut ce que vaut le salariat. Voilà ce dont Paul Valéry a été toute sa vie plus profondément averti que bien d'autres.

Car c'est ne rien comprendre que ne pas prendre en compte la duplicité fondamentale de la vie de Valéry et les rapports entre ses deux vies, celle matinale, prioritaire à tous égards, des *Cahiers,* où il s'astreint avec passion à l'exercice de l'intelligence d'une part, et celle des œuvres de commande et des mondanités où il s'autorise à être bête – dit-il – d'autre part. Il est facile – et raisonnable – d'en tirer la conclusion qu'au fond il n'accepte l'esthétique du résultat que comme une manière de gagner sa vie, c'est à dire comme une concession à l'utilitaire. Encore ne le fait-il que par nécessité pécuniaire, parce qu'il lui est parfois arrivé d'être pauvre au point de devoir produire sciemment de faux manuscrits de ses œuvres parce qu'ils se vendaient mieux et plus cher que ses œuvres publiées elles-mêmes.

Mais laissons là toute cette monnaie de singes, car la pensée de Valéry nous conduit à des conclusions d'une portée beaucoup plus vaste.

> J'ai voulu vous montrer comment cet art, loin d'être un futile divertissement, loin d'être une spécialité qui se borne à la production de quelques spectacles, à l'amusement des yeux qui le considèrent ou des corps qui s'y livrent, est tout simplement une poésie générale de l'action des êtres vivants
>
> *Philosophie de la danse* - P 40

Car oui, lecteur, tu as bien lu : ce qui est en jeu dans ce texte – timidement et comme subrepticement – c'est *une poésie générale de l'action des êtres vivants.* Et c'était bien le sens de cette remarque presque anodine pourtant où il identifiait au cœur même de la danse comme « *une manière de vie intérieure, en donnant à présent, à ce terme de psychologie, un sens nouveau où la **physiologie** domine?* ». Dès que l'on cesse de séparer l'esprit du corps, la danse et la pensée apparaissent pour ce qu'elles sont : une seule et même chose. C'est à dire *une poésie générale…*

Valéry – et il semble bien qu'en cela il soit jusqu'ici resté unique – envisage ici la dynamique des arts et de la pensée comme l'activité fondamentale, non pas d'une humanité étrangère à la nature et comme tombée du ciel, mais bien du vivant tout entier.

الرقص ـ التفكير

الرقص - التفكير

مددت الحبال من برج الجرس إلى برج الجرس؛ أكاليل من النافذة إلى النافذة؛ سلاسل ذهبية من نجم إلى نجم، وأنا أرقص

آرثر رامبو

ذريعة النص التالي هي مؤتمر عقده بول فاليري في 5 مارس 1936 في جامعة أناليس ونشر في كونفرانسيا في نوفمبر 1936. النص المستخدم هنا هو النص الذي نشرته إصدارات) Allia) . في عام 2023 تحت عنوان فلسفة الرقص ولا يسعنا إلا أن نأمل أن يتم تطبيق كلمات فاليري التمهيدية القليلة هنا. يجب أن تستسلم لسماع بعض التوقعات بأن الإنسان الذي لا يرقص سوف يخاطر بالرقص أمامك. ستنتظر قليلاً لحظة التعجب، وستقول في نفسك إنني لست أقل صبراً منك للاستمتاع بهذا. أدخل على الفور في أفكاري وسأخبرك دون مزيد من التحضير أن الرقص في رأيي لا يقتصر على كونه تمرينًا، أو ترفيهًا، أو فنًا للزينة، وأحيانًا لعبة في صالات الاستقبال؛ إنه أمر خطير، وفي جوانب معينة، أمر جليل للغاية

النمل لا يضيع دقيقة واحدة. العنكبوت يراقب ولا يلعب على شبكته. ولكن ماذا عن الإنسان ؟ الإنسان هو هذا الحيوان الفريد الذي يراقب نفسه بينما يحيا و يعطي لنفسه قيمة ويضع كل هذه القيمة التي يسعده أن يمنحها لنفسه في نفس المكان التي يعلقها على التصورات عديمة الفائدة والأفعال التي ليس لها عواقب جسدية وحيوية.

بول فاليري – فلسفة الرقص
Allia Paris 2023

يفترض فاليري – أو يخترع – أن الحيوانات ستكون مشغولة على الدوام ببقائها ... وقيل الشيء نفسه عن انسان ما قبل التاريخ، قبل أن يأتي كتاب اقتصاد العصر الحجري لمارشال سالينز ليعيد الاقتصاديين إلى الملاحظة والعقل ... بدلاً من ثقتهم العمياء في قصص الكتاب المقدس. وربما كانت بعض الملاحظات الإثنوغرافية كافية لو كان أهل الاقتصاد قادرين على تحمل عناء التأمل قبل إلقاء المواعظ على مواضيع لا يعرفون عنها شيئا أما بالنسبة للنمل، فنحن نعرف الآن كيف تسير الأمور على حقيقتها، وما لم يكن من الممكن أن يعرفه لافونتين: أن النمل يعطي انطباعًا بأنه موجود دائمًا في العمل، لكن هذا مجرد انطباع. إنهم يتجولون ويتجولون كثيرًا، وليسوا مجتهدين كثيرًا . ولذلك فإن الإنسان ليس بأي حال من الأحوال صانعًا لما لا فائدة منه، وبهذه الاستثنائية داخل العالم الحي يحاول بذلك رفع نفسه إلى ما هو أبعد من حالة الحيوانات الأخرى. يبدو أن معظم الناس، بما في ذلك العلماء في بعض الأحيان مهووسون بما يسمى الانتقاء الطبيعي - وهو في معظم الحالات تمثيل وهمي للمنافسة الرأسمالية - وقد نسوا أنه لكي يكون هناك اصطفاء طبيعي، فلا بد أن يكون هناك خلق طبيعي مسبقا، وإلا فإن الانتخاب سيحدث. لقد توقف منذ وقت طويل، لعدم وجود خصائص للاختيار

إنهم يخبروننا دائمًا عن دار-وين، لكنهم لا يخبروننا أبدًا بأي شيء عن دار-لوز كما قال أحد الأصدقاء مازحًا . في الواقع ان القدرات الإبداعية للكائنات الحية تتجاوز بكثير ما هو مفيد . وهذا من حسن الحظ . لأن ما هو مفيد لا يمكن تحديده إلا على أساس الظروف، سواء الحالية أو المتوقعة على المدى القصير . لكن على المدى الأطول، وعلى مقياس بضعة ملايين من السنين، تتجاوز الظروف بسرعة كبيرة قدرات الإنسان على التنبؤ والترقب... ولكن، كما يرى الجميع، حتى على مدى ملايين السنين، فإن الظروف لا تتجاوز بأي حال من الأحوال القدرات الإبداعية للكائنات الحية، باعتبارها نظامًا عالميًا، أي أبعد من الحالة الخاصة لكل نوع. لأن الحياة استمرت لنحو 3.5 مليار سنة، وهي مدة تفوق بكثير خيال البشر . الحياة كما أن البشر أنفسهم – مهما قالوا عنها – لا يعرفون على الإطلاق إلى أين تتجه. إنها لا تخرج من المشاكل إلا من خلال الإبداع الجامح، والذي من المرجح أن لا يكون لغالبيته أي فائدة من الناحية الإحصائية، وجزء صغير منه فقط يمكن أن يكون مفيدًا، في بعض الأحيان، في عمليات التكيف المحتملة. ولذلك إذا كان الإنسان مثل أي شيء آخر في الحياة هو في الواقع صانع لما لا فائدة منه، فإن هذا، كما رأينا للتو، لا يستبعد بأي حال من الأحوال ما لا فائدة منه، بل على العكس من ذلك هذا الفكر الذي يبنينا، في أعيننا، فوق حالتنا الحساسة، هو بالضبط [...] الفكر الذي لا يخدم أي غرض. [...] أفكارنا العميقة هي الأكثر لا مبالاة بالحفاظ علينا ، وبطريقة ما، عديمة الجدوى فيما يتعلق بهذا الحفاظ.

بول فاليري – فلسفة الرقص

حسنًا ، "غير مبال بالحفاظ علينا "؟ من أي وجهة نظر؟ فيما يتعلق بأي مقاييس زمنية؟ وفيما يتعلق بالحفاظ علينا ، هل هو الحفاظ على الأفراد أم الحفاظ على الأنواع؟ كل التفكير النفعي هو بالضرورة تفكير قصير المدى، تفكير قصير النظر، لأن المدى الطويل والطويل جدًا لا يمكن

44

تصوره، أي بعيدًا عن متناول أي تفكير. ولذلك، فإن "الفكرة التي لا فائدة منها"، بعيدًا عن كونها مجرد هدر هائل ـ وهو كذلك أيضًا بشكل واضح ـ تتشكل في الواقع، على الرغم من أنها ربما في غاية الصغر من وجهة نظر إحصائية، تمثل أملنا الوحيد في البقاء على المدى الطويل. ، حيث أنها محاولة لتجاوز حتى ما يمكن تخيله. هذا التجوال، هذه المخاطرة المجنونة حقًا، هذه الرحلة للعيش إلى ما وراء ما هو مفيد ، باختصار، هذه التكلفة والرفاهية المذهلة، هي في الواقع جوهر هذه القدرة الغريبة على الاستمرار في الحياة كلها التي تحملنا وبطبيعة الحال، فإن ما يبدو لنا، مع القليل من الإدراك المتأخر والمسافة، من خلال تنوع الظروف والأنواع، كنوع من طقوس العربدة الإبداعية للأحياء، لا يكون صالحًا إلا بقدر ما لا يتعارض مع الضرورة الأساسية للتكاثر، وتنوع الخصائص المتراكمة داخل كل فرد، وكذلك داخل كل نوع، ولا وحتى تراكم التنوع المطلوب للأنواع لمجابهة تنوع الظروف لكن فضولنا الذي كان أكثر حماسا دائما مما هو ضروري ونشاطنا الأكثر إثارة مما يتطلبه أي هدف حيوي تطور إلى اختراع الفنون والعلوم والمشكلات العالمية، واختراع إنتاج الأشياء والأشكال، والإجراءات التي يمكننا الاستغناء عنها بسهولة

بول فاليري ـ فلسفة الرقص

ويلمح فاليري ـ تقريبًا ـ إلى الضرورة البيولوجية لعدم الجدوى عندما ينظر إلى الفضول، وهو أكثر بكثير من مجرد قدرة بشرية، وهو يعلم جيدًا أن الحيوانات غير محرومة منه بوضوح. كما أنه يعلم جيدًا أيضًا أن كل فضول سواء كان حيوانيًا أو إنسانيًا هو بحكم تعريفه فضول زائد عن الحاجة أي أكثر من اللازم. وهذه هي الطريقة التي نتعرف بها عليه. ولكن بدلًا من فهم الفضول البشري باعتباره امتدادًا ـ متضخمًا بلا شك ـ لفضول حيواني أساسي سابق، أي فضول حيواني ناتج عن التطور البيولوجي والذي ينشأ منه فضول الإنسان على هذا النحو، وإلا سيكون غير مفهوم وكما لو أنه "سقط من السماء"، فاليري يركز (وهذا صحيح!) على عدم الجدوى الأساسية والجذرية للحضارات نفسها ومنتجاتها التي يمكننا الاستغناء عنها بسهولة. لماذا نكرس أنفسنا بحماس شديد لإنتاج الأشياء والأشكال والأفعال التي يمكننا الاستغناء عنها بسهولة؟ يعود هذا إلى جانب آخر يعود إليه فاليري غالباً ـ والذي سيكون من الضروري حقاً العودة إليه ـ وهو السمة الإدمانية الحقيقية للإبداع الفكري. الفن مثل العلم، كل حسب طريقته يميل إلى صنع نوع مفيد من عدم الفائدة، نوع من الضروري، من الاعتباطي. وبالتالي، فإن الإبداع الفني ليس إبداعًا للأعمال بقدر ما هو خلق الحاجة إلى الأعمال [...]

فلسفة الرقص

إذا وافقنا - على مضض وبشكل مؤقت للغاية - على قبول الفصل الذي أقامه فاليري بين منتج ومستهلك الإبداع الفكري في كتابه

(Cours de Poétique au Collège de France)

فيجب علينا أن نأخذ في الاعتبار الإدمان الناجم عن الإبداع الفكري وفقًا لـ هذين الجانبين، جانب الإنتاج وجانب الاستهلاك. ومن هذا المنظور، يبدو الرقص لفاليري كما لنا كمثال نقي للغاية لعملية إدمان المنتج، الذي تفلت حركته مما نسميه الواقع، أي كل فهم متفق عليه بشكل عام للواقع.
الراقصة في عالم آخر، لم تعد تلك التي نرسمها بأعيننا، بل ذلك الذي [...] تنسجه بخطواتها وتبنيه بإيماءاتها. لكن في هذا العالم لا يوجد هدف خارجي للأفعال؛ لا يوجد شيء للاستيلاء عليه، أو الانضمام إليه، أو دفعه بعيدًا، أو الفرار منه ، وهو شيء يكمل الفعل تمامًا ويعطي الحركات أولًا اتجاهًا وتنسيقًا خارجيًا، ومن ثم نتيجة واضحة ومؤكدة

– بول فاليري – فلسفة الرقص

من المؤكد أن حركة الراقص تنفلت من أي هدف خارجي – في الأفعال – لجسد الراقص وعقله، لكن فاليري من نفس الحركة يكشف لنا سرًا لا يعرفه إلا علماء الرياضيات الذين ابتكروا المفاهيم الجديدة للهندسة في النهاية كان من الممكن أن تكشف لنا أعمال القرن التاسع عشر - على سبيل المثال هنري بوانكاريه - لو كانت لدينا الجرأة لقراءتها هذا السر وهو أن الفضاء ليس هذه الاستمرارية الفارغة واللامتناهية التي خلقها نيوتن (وبشكل أعم في القرن السابع عشر) من العدم، ولكنه على العكس من ذلك محدد (مبني) من خلال مجموعات من التحولات (أي التدوير، والترجمات، وما إلى ذلك)التي تعمل فيه وبعبارة أخرى، الفضاء ليس شيئا معطى في حد ذاته. إنه ليس مثل نوع من المسرح الموجود مسبقًا والذي يمكن أن تُدرج فيه حياتنا وإيماءاتنا، ولكنه - على المستوى الحدسي على

الأقل ـ هو على العكس من ذلك، منسوج ومبني من خلال أفعالنا وإيماءاتنا.

انظر الفصل الثالث في

Pourquoi l'espace a 3 Dimensions Dernières Pensées 1917-1913.هنري بوانكاريه ـ فلاماريون

وبشكل أكثر دقة، يوضح بوانكاريه أن حدسنا للفضاء يعتمد بشكل أساسي على مفهوم الحركة. على الإدراك الداخلي ـ العضلي ـ لحركات أجسادنا هذا هو النهج الذي يجعل كلمات ماركس يتردد صداها بشكل غريب: في ديناميكيات الرقص، ينهار الفرق بين التفسير والتحويل لأن الفضاء الذي يتم استحضاره ثم خلقه من خلال حركة الراقصة، يجد نفسه مفسرًا ومحولًا في نفس الوقت، أو بشكل أكثر دقة، مفسرًا. لأنه تحول بالأفعال. وهذا يكشف لنا أن معنى كلمة تفسير في جملة ماركس لم يكن يهدف إلا إلى تفسير مجرد، أي غير مجرب جسديا، وبالتالي بطريقة معينة، كما سنشير لاحقا، غير راقص. كما يوضح بوانكاريه أن الفضاء ليس هذا المطلق الفارغ الذي تحدث عنه نيوتن، ولكنه نسبي في الأساس وأعني بهذا ليس فقط أننا يمكن أن ننتقل إلى منطقة أخرى من الفضاء دون أن ندرك ذلك (وهذا بالفعل ما يحدث لأننا لا نلاحظ انتقال الأرض)، وليس فقط أنه يمكن زيادة جميع أبعاد الأشياء وبنفس النسبة دون أن نتمكن من معرفتها، بشرط أن تشارك أدوات القياس لدينا في هذا التوسع؛ ولكنني أريد أيضًا أن أقول إن الفضاء يمكن أن يتشوه وفقًا لقانون اعتباطي، بشرط أن يتم تشويه أدوات القياس الخاصة بنا بدقة وفقًا لنفس القانون

هنري بوانكاريه، أفكار أخيرة
ص62-61

ويحدد بعد ذلك مباشرة أن ما يعنيه بـ«القانون التعسفي» هو تحريف مستمر وبالتالي، فإن الفضاء، الذي يُنظر إليه بشكل مستقل عن أدوات مقايسنا ، ليس له خصائص مترية أو إسقاطية؛ لديه فقط خصائص طوبولوجية. وهو غير متبلور، أي أنه لا يختلف عما يمكن استنتاجه من أي تشوه مستمر

هنري بوانكاريه، أفكار أخيرة
ص62

نشعر على الفور بمدى قرب هذه الرؤية للفضاء، الذي يُنظر إليه على أنه قابل للتشوه، من رؤية الزمكان القابل للتشوه في النظرية النسبية ـ التي شارك بوانكاريه أيضًا في تطويرها إلى حد كبيرلذلك يشرح لنا بوانكاريه أن هناك شيئًا ما وراء الفضاء المعتاد، شيئًا أعمق، وهو ما يسمح لعالم الرياضيات بالتفكير بشكل صحيح حتى يمكنه البناءً على أرقام سيئة الصنع .

(Dernières Pensées، P59-70)

وهو المجال الذي يشمله نظام الرياضيات وهذا ما يسمى الآن دراسة الطوبولوجيا ، والتي تبين أنها دراسة الفضاء غير المتبلور، أي بدون أشكال ـ لأنه يمكن تشويهها حسب الرغبة ولكن بعد ذلك، وبالعودة إلى راقصة ڤاليري، يتم طرح السؤال حول طبيعة المادة قبل خلق المساحة التي تنسجها الراقصة وتبنيها بخطواتها وإيماءاتها. من الواضح أن الأمر لا يتعلق بمكان، لأن الفضاء هو بالتحديد الراقص الذي يخلقه وما زلنا نعيش بالنسبة للجزء الأكبر منا مع فكرة الفضاء اللامتناهي وهي فكرة متناقضة إلى حد ما دون أن نشك في ما يمكن أن يحمله هذا التمثيل باعتباره دينيًا، أي إرهابيًا على وجه التحديد.

49

وكما يتضح من هذا الاكتشاف المؤلم من **بليز باسكال**، على خلفية تجواله اللاهوتي، "فإن الصمت الأبدي لهذه المساحات اللامتناهية يخيفني ...".
وهو ما تجيب عليه فكرة الطيب جاستون باشلار دون أي ارتعاش:
" أنا لا أعيش في اللانهاية، لأنه في اللانهاية، لا يكون المرء في بيته".
كاشفًا بذلك أن دور ووظيفة كل هذه اللانهائيات ليس لها في الواقع أي سبب آخر للوجود سوى طردنا من منازلنا، من عالمنا. لتجعلنا غرباء دائمين ومن ناحية أخرى، في الهندسة الجديدة التي تكشفها لنا الرياضيات ويكشفها لنا الرقص، نحن في موطننا بشكل لا يمكن القضاء عليه لأن حركاتنا وأفعالنا هي التي تنسج وتبني الفضاء، الذي لا يمكن أن يوجد خلفه سوى ما أسماه أناكسيماندر "أبيرون"، أي "الخالي من المحيط" (المصطلحان يشتركان في نفس الجذر الاشتقاقي "محيط")، أي غير محدد ولكنه ليس غير محدود بالمعنى المعتاد للكلمة. وبطبيعة الحال، إذا أخذنا الأمر حرفيًا فإن اللامحدود يعني بلا حدود ولكنه يعني بعد ذلك عدم وجود حد وهو ما لا علاقة له بأي نوع من اللانهاية. إذا لم يتم ترسيم أرض جيراني ، فمن الصحيح أن نقول إن أرض جيراني بلا حدود. لكن لن يستنتج أحد من هذا أنه غير محدود بمعنى اللانهائي. علاوة على ذلك، إذا لم تظهر أرض جيراني نتيجة للإغفال في السجل العقاري فهي غير محددة، ، لكنها بالتالي ليست لا نهائية. إذا ترجمنا كلمة "بدقة"، "حرفيًا"، أو كلمة
"Apeiron"إلى غير محدود بالمعنى المعتاد للامحدود، ثم بشكل عكسي، لدي الحق في الادعاء بأنه إذا كان الله غير محدود فذلك لأنه لم يكتمل تمامًا، الأمر الذي ربما سينتهي بأن اكتسب تحفظ معظم اللاهوتيين وبعبارة أخرى
(Apeiron)
لا تعني غير محدود أو لانهائي. اللانهاية التي علاوة على ذلك في كل مكان ودائمًا، لا تكشف عن نفسها أبدًا على أنها أي شيء آخر غير التكرار الذي لا نهاية له.

وبعد ذلك، إذا لم نجعل من ثقافة الجهل طريقة مناسبة لاستكشاف أسرار الواقع، فقد يصبح من الخداع الفكري عدم الأخذ بعين الاعتبار النتائج التي توصل إليها عالم الرياضيات جورج كانتور، والتي تفيد بوجود أنواع مختلفة من اللانهائيات، كبيرة وصغيرة، والتي يمكنها بطريقة أو بأخرى أن تتداخل مع بعضها البعض... وبالتالي فإن مجموعة الأعداد الصحيحة الطبيعية لا نهائية بطريقتها الخاصة (قابلة للعد)، ولكن يمكن تضمينها - وهي مدرجة بشكل عام - في مجموعة الأعداد الحقيقية ، وهي أيضًا لا نهائية، ولكن بطريقة مختلفة وفريدة تمامًا، نظرًا لأن مجموعة الأعداد لا تقل لا نهائية عن 1 و 0الحقيقية المتضمنة (على سبيل المثال) بين مجموعة جميع الأعداد الحقيقية في مجملها، والتي يمكن أن تبدو واضحة تمامًا بشكل مذهل لكننا لم نصل إلى نهاية الدوار لأن كانتور يوضح أيضًا أنه لا يوجد المزيد من العناصر في فضاء البعد

N

(هو عدد صحيح منتهٍ)

1 و0أكثر من الأعداد الحقيقية بين

((أو في المجموعة الكاملة للأعداد الحقيقية

وفي مواجهة هذا الدليل (الرياضي)، فوجئ كانتور باكتشافه لدرجة أنه كتب: "أنا أرى ذلك، لكنني لا أصدقه"

ما تكشفه اكتشافات كانتور في هذه الحالة هو أنه عندما نتحدث عن فضاء حرف فإننا نتحدث فقط عن بنية معينة لمجموعة لا حصر لها N ذي البعد ليس الأكبر" من عدد عناصر الفضاء " N من العناصر التي يكون عددها على سبيل المثال، هي مجموعة الأعداد 1. لكن مساحة البعد 1البعد الحقيقية نفسها، التي تتوافق فقط مع بنية معينة (بنية البديهيات التي تصنع الأعداد الحقيقية) لمجموعة لا نهائية، على سبيل المثال، مجموعة من "الحجم الكبير" - يكون حجمها أكبر بأي حال من الأحوال من حجم المجموعة اللانهائية من الأعداد الصحيحة الطبيعية.

لكن هذه الهياكل المختلفة هي قيود (كما يقول علماء الطبيعة)، والتي تحدد وتعرف الأشكال داخل أو خارج الأبيرون. النماذج التي تسمح لنا بطريقة ما باستكشاف بعض الأجزاء الصغيرة مما يخرج من نطاق الابيرون. باختصار يسير الراقص الرياضي بنفس الطريقة التي يتبعها راقص ڤاليري. إنه يقوم بإيماءات (تقوم بتطوير البديهيات، والتعريفات، والإثباتات، والنظريات)، وإيماءات فكرية، بالطبع، لكنها مجرد إيماءات على الرغم من ذلك، وهذه الإيماءات تنسج وتبني... ليس الفضاء، بالطبع لا، ولكن الرياضيات. في رؤية أناكسيماندر، فإن الأبيرون نفسه هو في أي لحظة، النشاط الذي يولد جميع الأشكال، المعدنية أو النباتية أو الحيوانية. أو البشر – وإبداعاتهم – كمجرد حالة خاصة ومن ثم فبدلاً من اتباع تعرجات هايدجر بينما نخون أناكسيماندر جزئيًا – وببهجة – نفضل هنا تفسير أبيرون من الزاوية الصينية للطاو، باعتباره هذا غير المحدد الذي تحررت منه جميع الأشكال. أو إذا فضلنا الأشياء بهذه الطريقة، تحت زخارف الفراغ الكمي، الذي هو مبدع تمامًا كما يقال عن الطاو. أو حتى "مثل "فم الظل

هذا الذي تحدث عنه فيكتور هوجو في

Les Contemplations

وهذا ما يسمح لڤاليري بمقارنة الرقص بالأحلام والتحدث عن عمل الراقص. لا يوجد شيء خارج النظام الذي تشكله الراقصة لنفسها من خلال أفعالها، وهو النظام الذي يجعلنا نفكر في النظام المعاكس تمامًا وليس الأقل انغلاقًا الذي يشكله النوم بالنسبة لنا، والذي يكون قانونه المعاكس تمامًا هو الإلغاء والامتناع التام عن أي أفعال.

فلسفة الرقص29ص

هذه ملاحظة يمكن من خلالها التعرف على اشمئزاز ڤاليري من الأحلام. الحلم... ككلمة يولي ڤاليري هنا عناية كبيرة للتحايل عليها من خلال الإشارة إلى النوم.

ولكنه جهد ضائع، إذ لا النوم ولا الأحلام تظهر الامتناع التام عن الأفعال. ويكفي أن نلاحظ الحركات الخفية التي يقوم بها قط أو كلب يحلم، أو حتى ببساطة أكثر تلك التي يقوم بها الإنسان النائم . التالي في متناول اليد، لفهم ما نفتقر إليه بشكل غريب هنا في تصورات فاليري، وهو فهم العقل كما هو . كنشاط محاكاة لأننا نعلم الآن — وعلمياً — أنه لا الحركات ولا الأفعال تغيب عن الأحلام. نحن نعلم أنهم حاضرون في الأحلام، كمحاكاة مكبوتة، وأنه يحدث أحيانًا أن تهرب إلى الواقع، من النوم ومن الأحلام، من هذا الامتناع التام المفترض عن الأفعال، الذي يتحدث عنه فاليري.

مع ذلك، في الواقع، ما يبدو أنه في قلب ملاحظة فاليري أعلاه هو بالأحرى فكرة الإغلاق، ديناميكية الراقصة التي تنغلق على النظام الذي تشكله لنفسها من خلال أفعالها . إذن فإن ما يشير إليه هذا الإغلاق هو هذا الأبيرون الذي يشكل ما بعد حركاته . غير المعين وغير المحدد و الذي لا يتكون حتى من مكان، لأن الفضاء هو ما تحيكه وتبنيه أفعال الراقصة في كل لحظة، وبما أن حركاتها لم تحدد وتعرف بعد أي شيء خارج هذا الأبيرون، الذي يبدو بالتالي على ما هو عليه . : غياب الفضاء

لكن هذا النظام الذي يشكله الراقص لنفسه يقودنا إلى "أبيرون" آخر . لأن هذا النظام الذي يشكله الراقص يجب أن يأتي في حد ذاته من نظام آخر غير محدد، من نظام داخلي آخر غير محدد، تظهر تموجات النسيج فيه، وتتطور، وتختفي في أي لحظة داخل جسد الراقص وعقله، والتي تشكل مصدر تصرفاته لذلك، إذا اعترفنا، مسلحين بالضربة القاضية لمالارميه، بأن "كل تفكير يحدث نتيجة لضربة ديس"، فيجب علينا بعد ذلك أن نعترف بأن الأمر نفسه ينطبق على أفعال الراقص التي تظهر فقط، كما تفعل أفكارنا. وتبرز على خلفية الصدفة. لذلك، بالإضافة للابيرون الخارجي الذي حددناه بالفعل، يجب علينا الآن إضافة ابيرون باطني آخر، غير محدد هذه المرة ومن النقطة التي نقف فيها الآن، من خلال الوسيط العقلي لزجاجة كلاين -

وهو جسم معروف جيدًا باطنه هو نفسه مظهره الخارجي أيضًا ـ يمكننا أن نشك في أنه في هذه المسألة، فإن الأبيرون الخارجي والأبيرون الداخلي هما شيء واحد ولكن بعد أن حاولنا بمكر قلب عقل القارئ البائس رأسًا على عقب ومن الداخل إلى الخارج، دعونا نتفحص العالم العملي

الانسان العملي هو انسان لديه غريزة الاقتصاد في الوقت والوسائل، ويحصل عليه بسهولة أكبر لأن هدفه أكثر وضوحًا وأفضل موضعًا: كائن خارجي. الرقص هو عكس ذلك تماماً. [...] ليس هناك في حد ذاته، أي سبب، ولا ميل محدد للاكتمال فيه . ويجب ألا تحتوي صيغة الرقص الخالص على ما يدل على نهايته

فلسفة الرقص ـ ص 31

إن حجم عقل الإنسان العملي يتحدد بحجم الشيء الخارجي الذي يطمع فيه، مع وجود الهامش العقلي الزائد اللازم للتعامل مع الصعوبات والأمور غير القابلة للقياس في الطريق الذي يفصله عن هدفه، ولكن ليس أكثر. . بطريقة أو بأخرى، فإن انتباهه، وإحساسه بالملاحظة، ومسار أفكاره، وحتى خياله، يجد نفسه متقلصًا، ومقيدًا بالمسعى الذي يسعى إليه

وبمجرد أن يحقق هدفه، ينهار التوتر الذي كان يحركه ويواجه فجأة نوعًا غريبًا من الفراغ. وبعد أن كان انسان العمل المثير للإعجاب إلى هذا الحد أو ذاك ـ أو اعتقد أنه كان كذلك ـ حتى ذلك الحين، يجد نفسه الآن وقد تراجع إلى رتبة مغرور . إن تحقيق هدفه لا يكمل سعيه فحسب، بل يكمل الانسان أيضًا لبعض الوقت. حتى لو كان قد وضع لنفسه هدف أن يصبح إمبراطورًا، فقد حقق هدفه، فهو متقدم جدًا . بعد أن امتلك كل القوى، عليه أن يختبرها في أسرع وقت ممكن، وبالتالي يتخيل على الفور شيئًا يرغب فيه، ويفضل أن يكون شيئًا تعسفيًا، من أجل إظهار حريته المستردة بعد تحقيق هدفه.

يمكن لأي شيء أن يفعل الخدعة نفسها، ولكن عندما يتم استدعاؤه للظهور، فإن هذا الشيء يرفض أن يؤتي ثماره. إن التعسفي، الذي يتم استدعاؤه لإظهار نفسه، يرفض القيام بذلك، وحتى داخل عقل الإمبراطور، تستمر الروح في النفخ فقط متى وأينما تريد وهكذا فإن راقصة أخرى مثل سالومي بعد أن رقصت بشكل رائع في مأدبة هيرودس، يعرض عليها الملك المبهر "ما تريد، حتى لو كان نصف مملكته". بالكاد خرجت الفتاة الصغيرة من خيالها في تصميم الرقصات، ولا تريد شيئًا، باستثناء الاستمرار في رقصها أو استئنافه. ثم تلجأ إلى والدتها هيروديا وتسألها: "ماذا أريد؟". سؤال لا يملك الإمبراطور الجديد بالتأكيد إمكانية طرحه على والدته علنًا. الراقصة، التي يخبرنا عنها فاليري، تمامًا مثل سالومي في الحكاية، ليس لها هدف خارجي. لكن الحقيقة هي أنها ليس لديها هدف داخلي أيضًا. حركاتها تبرز الفضاء، وتظهره كفضاء من قلب هذه اللحظة الشعرية العمودية التي يتحدث عنها جاستون باشلار. ولأنها عمودية، فإن هذه اللحظة ليس لها – ولا تريد أي – بداية أو نهاية. وهذا لا يعني بأي حال من الأحوال أنها "خارج الزمن". لا يزال الوقت مناسبًا، لكن هذه المرة أصبحت عمودية. ولم تعد تتناسب مع التسلسل المعتاد – الواقعي – للأحداث. الذي لم يعد يمر، بل يفقس، بل يتطور إلى بُعد زمني مختلف. إنه نوع من الزمن الذي يخلق نفسه ويحافظ على نفسه، نوع من الطيران المنزلق للزمن الذي اختفت منه كل خفقات الأجنحة. زمن خالٍ من الضوضاء، حيث يتدفق وحده بصمت، التدفق من فم الظل لهوجو

يا زمن أوقف طيرانك يقول لامارتين من على حافة بحيرة يتذكرها" "
ويضيف كبداية للبطء الشعري: "أقول لهذه الليلة: كوني أبطأ". وهنا نجد هذا الإدمان على زمن الإبداع الفكري الذي تحدثنا عنه أعلاه ولكن لعدم وجود هدف، فإن الراقصة لديها مع ذلك حياة داخلية، وحتى حياة داخلية مكثفة ذات نسيج ضيق بشكل خاص، على وجه التحديد لأنها ليس لديها هدف

لذا اسمح لي ببعض التعبير الجريء، ألا يمكننا أن نأخذ هذا في الاعتبار، وقد جعلتك تشعر به بالفعل، كطريقة للحياة الداخلية، من خلال إعطاء هذا المصطلح في علم النفس معنى جديدًا حيث يهيمن علم وظائف الأعضاء

32فلسفة الرقص/ص

ورغم أن بول فاليري كان يعتبر في أغلب الأحيان "رجل العقل" إلا أننا نرى من هذه الملاحظة أنه ـ على عكس المتدينين والفلاسفة ـ يدرك الوحدة الأساسية للجسد والروح، وأنه يدركها في حقيقتها الفعلية ، أي في "ديناميكيتها لأنه يسمي هذه الوحدة "طوق الأصداء

يشار هنا إلى ما يسمى في العلوم الحالية بالتخدير، أي المجموعة الفرعية من الجهاز العصبي التي تسمح بالإدراك الديناميكي للجسد بناءً على المعلومات التي طورتها عشرات الملايين من أجهزة الاستشعار من حوالي عشرة أنواع مختلفة موزعة في جميع أنحاء الجسد. فيما يتعلق بالرقص فهو على وجه التحديد مجموعتان فرعيتان من التخدير المرتبط بالإدراك الداخلي للحركات، وهما الحس الباطني والحركي في حالة الأنشطة الجسدية والفكرية مثل الرقص والموسيقى والرياضة، ولكن أيضًا العديد من الأنشطة الأخرى. أيضا تقترن التصورات الداخلية والتصورات الخارجية ديناميكيًا في جميع الأوقات لتمكين تنفيذ أي إجراء وخاصة أي تصحيحات يتم إجراؤها على النشاط و أي تقدم للحركات. ولهذا السبب كان فاليري حادًا بشكل مدهش حين تحدث عن الرنين، وهو مصطلح أكثر دقة وأوضح في النهاية من مصطلح الاقتران المعتاد. خطوة أخرى في هذا الاتجاه سنجد أنفسنا أمام هذا المفهوم البوذي للوعي كما أوضحه عالم الأحياء فرانسيسكو فاريلا في بعض النصوص، وهذا يعني أنه إحساس إضافي للحواس الأخرى والذي لن يكون في النهاية سوى شيء آخر. (ديناميكي!) أي إدراك النشاط الإدراكي للحواس الأخرى

أي تصور الإدراك باختصار. وهذا يعني شيئًا قريبًا جدًا من نوع الرنين الذي تحدث عنه فاليري أعلاه.وتبقى الحقيقة أن الوعي ليس فكرًا. وإلى جانب ذلك، فإن العكس ليس أقل صحة. الوعي ــ بطبيعة الحال وفقًا لما قلناه للتو ــ هو في الأساس إدراك. أما الفكر، من ناحية أخرى، فهو يتعلق بالعمل. يجمع الفكر ويتلاعب ويلعب ويعيد عرض النماذج التي يبنيها ويكيفها باستمرار، ويتجول في محاكاة ليست واعية في معظمها. هذا ما تظهره الأحلام ــ بمجرد أن نتوقف عن البحث عن المعنى فيها ونركز أولاً على الطريقة التي تقدم بها نفسها. إن المحاكاة التي تقدمها لنا الأحلام مثالية ودقيقة جدًا ـ بما أنها لا تتعارض مع التصورات الخارجية أو الداخلية ـ لدرجة أننا نعتقد أننا موجودون. وفي بعض الأحيان، تكون الانطباعات حية وعنيفة جدًا لدرجة أننا نفضل عدم تصديقها.

ومع ذلك، لا يزال هناك لغز لا يقوله فاليري ، لكن عالم الرياضيات هنري بوانكاريه يحاول مواجهته في الفصل الثالث بعنوان الاختراع الرياضي في كتابه العلم والمنهج: أنواع الوعي. في لحظة معينة، لا يقدم لنا الوعي في وقت واحد جميع المعلومات التي تطورها حواسنا وتقدمها لنا. وينطبق الشيء نفسه، وفقًا لبوانكاريه، على الفكر الواعي، الذي ينتقي ما هو مناسب ضمن تموج في النسيج وتقزح الألوان لنشاط التفكير اللاواعي الأساسي. يقول فاليري، بصفته تلميذًا جيدًا لمالارميه، إن "كل فكر يبعث رمية نرد" وبالتالي فإن الفكر يعتمد على الصدفة، سواء من حيث مصادره أو من حيث حركته. يحاول بوانكاريه الخروج من هذا الوضع من خلال افتراض أن مبدأ اختيار ما يصل في نهاية المطاف إلى الوعي في الرياضيات هو الجمال ـ وهو الأمر الذي لا يحل الكثير، باستثناء تحديد ما يتكون منه الجمال، والذي لا يكاد يكون أقل شائكة. لكن بوانكاريه، الذي يتمتع بالخبرة في الأخذ في الاعتبار ضخامة التوافقيات والفرص التي تنطوي عليها، يدرك جيدًا أنه لم ينته من المشكلة بعد.

علاوة على ذلك لا يبدو أن السريالية أثارت بالفعل مسألة ديناميكيات الفكر. لقد كانت في أغلب الأحيان مكتفية بجمع الأعاجيب، وهي النتائج التي انتهى بها الأمر بإطلاق لفظ الأتمتة ، بدلاً من فهم واستيعاب الحركات الأساسية التي أدت إلى ظهور الأعاجيب. لكن في الواقع، لم يكن الأداء الحقيقي للفكر آليًا، ولا يمكن أن يكون بأي حال من الأحوال كذلك ، لأن الحياة ليست تلقائية، ولا الفكر كذلك، سواء كان واعيًا أو غير واع

يمكننا أن نتنبأ بالحدود الافتتاحية لمجال البحث السريالي من تعريفه الأولي للغاية: "التعبير عن الأداء الحقيقي للفكر". ليس التحقيق العاطفي والمثير في الأداء الحقيقي للفكر، وديناميكياته، ولكن فقط التعبير عنه. أما بالنسبة لديناميكيات الفكر، فقد كان الحل الجاهز موجودًا بالفعل، ومتوفرًا. يبدو أن التحليل النفسي، الذي ادعى أنه يقدم تفسيرًا لكل شيء ، كان كافيًا فيما يتعلق بتوفير فهم لديناميات العقل، والقضاء عليها في مهدها، إذا جاز التعبير، على كل ما كان يمكن أن يؤدي إلى أبعد وأعمق لكن لنعد إلى نموذج الرقص الذي اقترحه ڤاليري.. كيف يتم اختيار حركات الراقص؟ بالطبع، تقدم لنا الراقصة، جزئيًا، ما تعرف كيف تفعله: الحركات التي تعلمتها والتي ربما تؤديها وفقًا لخيوط تقليد معين. لكن كل حركة تحتوي على عنصر المخاطرة، وبالتالي عنصر الارتجال الذي لا يمكن علاجه. وينطبق الشيء نفسه على أي تفسير. لا يعزف الممثل نفس المقطوعة كل ليلة، ولا يعزف الموسيقي نفس المقطوعة في كل مرة لكن، اقتداءً بڤاليري، يجب علينا هنا أن نترك هذا السؤال مفتوحًا لعدم قدرتنا على توضيح ما يجب أن نسميه، سر، أو حتى معجزة أو بادرة إن بناء الكون أسهل بكثير من شرح كيف يقف الإنسان على قدميه. اسأل أرسطو وديكارت ولايبنتز وآخرين

فلسفة الرقص – ص 19

يعمم فاليري في اتجاه آخر مهم للغاية ويشير إلى أن الحس الباطني هو أيضًا أساس التعلم والتعليم والتطوير وبالتالي فهو يشارك في جميع الفنون. حاولت أن أنقل لكم فكرة مجردة إلى حد ما عن الرقص، وأن أمثلها لكم قبل كل شيء كفعل يتم استنتاجه، ثم ينبثق من فعل عادي ومفيد، ويعارضه في النهاية. لكن وجهة النظر العامة هذه (وهذا هو سبب اعتمادها اليوم)، تقودنا إلى اعتناق ما هو أكثر بكثير من الرقص نفسه. وكل عمل لا يتجه إلى المفيد، ويكون في المقابل قابلاً للتعلم والتحسين والتطوير في اتجاه الارتباط بهذا النوع المبسط من الرقص، وبالتالي يمكن اعتبار جميع الفنون حالات خاصة من الرقص. هذه الفكرة العامة، إذ أن جميع الفنون، بحكم تعريفها، تتضمن جزءًا من هذا الفعل، وهو الفعل الذي ينتج العمل أو الذي يظهره. [...]

33-34فلسفة الرقص -ص

وها هو يوسع على الفور ما أسسه للتو فيما يتعلق بالفنون إلى الشعر نفسه أي البدء في قول الآيات الشعرية يعني الدخول في رقصة لفظية
فلسفة الرقص – ص34

وحتى وسائل وتقنيات الشعر تعتبر من أشكال الرقص فما هي الاستعارة، إن لم تكن نوعا من الدوران للفكرة التي نجمع بها الصور المختلفة أو الأسماء المختلفة؟ وما هي كل هذه الصور التي نستخدمها، كل هذه الوسائل، مثل القوافي، والانقلابات، والأضداد، إذا لم تكن استخدامات لجميع إمكانيات اللغة، التي تفصلنا عن العالم العملي لنشكل نحن أيضًا عالمنا الخاص، أي المكان المميز للرقص الباطني

فلسفة الرقص - ص 41

وها هو أيضا يقوده إلى مفهوم الشعر باعتباره رقصًا لكنه يذهب إلى أبعد من ذلك بكثير ويحدد الخطوط العريضة لجماليات العملية الإبداعية، وجماليات الحركة، على عكس الجماليات التقليدية للنتيجة تمامًا. بين النشاط الإبداعي، أي العملية الإبداعية نفسها، والأعمال الفنية، والنتائج التي تم إنشاؤها وربما القابلة للتسويق، اتخذ فاليري على الفور - قدر الإمكان ـ نفس الاختيار الذي حدده مع ليوناردو دافنشي وفي مقدمته لطريقة ليوناردو دافنشي؛ فينشي، الذي غالبًا ما كان يفضل حركة فكره على إكمال أعماله، التي صادف أنه قد انهاها ـ وأحيانًا لا.

جميع الفنون هي أشكال متنوعة جدًا من الفعل ويتم تحليلها من حيث [...] الفعل. [...] يمكنك بعد ذلك أن تتصور إنشاء عمل فني، ربما رسم أو نحت، باعتباره عملا فنيا في حد ذاته. إن الشيء المادي الذي يتشكل تحت أصابع الفنان ليس أكثر من ذريعة، وإكسسوار المسرح، وموضوع الباليه هذا الرأي يبدو جريئا بالنسبة لك، على ما أتصور نعم ؟ لكن تذكر أنه بالنسبة للعديد من الفنانين العظماء، فإن العمل لا ينتهي أبدًا؛ إن ما يعتقدون أنه رغبتهم في الكمال ربما يكون مجرد شكل من أشكال هذه الحياة الباطنية المكونة من الطاقة والحساسية في التبادل وكما لو كان قابلاً للانعكاس

فلسفة الرقص - ص 38

وباعتبار العمل الفني المكتمل ذريعة بسيطة لحركة أساسية جدًا في العملية الإبداعية... من المحتمل أن يؤدي ذلك إلى تفجير التقليد بأكمله، والبنية الاجتماعية بأكملها التي يقوم عليها سوق الفن. لأن عملية الإبداع الفكري بعيدة المنال مثل أصغر لحظات الحياة. يمكنك أن تحضر وتسجل عرض راقص في وقت فراغك، لكن هذا لا يتيح لك الوصول إلى الحياة الباطنية للراقصة التي أنجبت هذا الأداء. نحن نسجل الرماد فقط، وهذا الرماد ليس نارًا. نعتقد أننا قادرون على أسر الفريسة، حين لا نتمكن من الإمساك ولو بظلها.

ونفس الحال في الفنون. إن العمل الفني، مهما كان ثمنه في نهاية المطاف، لا يتيح بأي حال من الأحوال إمكانية الوصول إلى سنوات من الصدفة والتأمل، أو إلى الأفكار المتعرجة - وحتى الكسل حيثما ينطبق ذلك - أو على العكس من ذلك، إلى ومضات لحظية وعربدة فورية، والتي أدى في نهاية المطاف إلى ما ليس له حتى أثر، إلى ما هو في نهاية المطاف دائما نتيجة سيئة .وهذا هو السبب في أن جميع المعارض تذهب سدى. تستمر الأيديولوجية - التي هي في الواقع مجرد شكل من أشكال الرقابة - في الإيحاء للجمهور بأن الجوهر موجود في العمل الفني، ومن المفترض أن يكون كافيًا في حد ذاته. العمل الفني الأصلي بالطبع، ليس نسخة مبتذلة بأي حال من الأحوال. لكن الأصل والنسخة متساويان، وهما في الحقيقة شيء واحد... مظهر من مظاهر العدم عند نقله إلى مجال أكثر اعتيادية، تفترض هذه الأيديولوجية أن البضائع الموجودة في واجهة المتجر سيكون لها وجود مستقل، وأن لحظات - أو حياة كاملة - من عمل البشر الذين بنوها ستعتبر لاغية وباطلة. ومن الواضح ما هي المصالح التي تخدمها مثل هذه الرؤية، حتى لو ادعى أتباعها، في بعض الأحيان، أنهم فوضويون فخورون.ومن غير الممكن إصلاح الحياة الحقيقية في مكان آخر، ولا يمكن بيعها فقط تظل الحقيقة أنه في هذا العالم المتدني — المتدني للغاية — لا يزال يتعين على الفنان، لسوء الحظ، أن يكسب رزقه، وأن الشهرة في هذه اللعبة تساوي ما يساوي الراتب. وهذا ما كان بول فاليري يدركه بعمق طوال حياته أكثر من كثيرين آخرين.لأنه ليس من المفهوم أن لا نأخذ في الاعتبار الازدواجية الأساسية في حياة فاليري اليومية والعلاقات بين حياتيه، الصباح، حياة المجلدات (غير المنشورة)، مع الأولوية العليا في جميع النواحي، حيث ينخرط بشغف في أعلى ممارسة للذكاء من ناحية، وفي الأعمال التكليفية والشؤون الدنيوية حيث يسمح لنفسه بأن يكون غبيًا - كما يقول - من ناحية أخرى. ومن السهل - والمعقول - أن نستنتج أنه في أعماقه، لا يقبل إلا جماليات النتيجة كوسيلة لكسب عيشه، أي كامتياز للمنفعة.

ومع ذلك فهو لا يفعل ذلك إلا بدافع الضرورة المالية، لأنه كان في بعض الأحيان فقيرًا جدًا لدرجة أنه اضطر إلى إنتاج مخطوطات مزيفة لأعماله عن علم، لأنها تباع بشكل أفضل.ولكن دعونا نترك كل هذه الأعمال القردية هناك، لأن تفكير فاليري يقودنا إلى استنتاجات ذات نطاق أوسع بكثير. أردت أن أوضح لك كيف أن هذا الفن، بعيدًا عن كونه ترفيهًا عديم الجدوى، وبعيدًا عن كونه تخصصًا يقتصر على إنتاج عدد قليل من العروض، لتسلية العيون التي تراه أو الأجساد التي تقوم به، هو بكل بساطة شعر عام عن عمل الكائنات الحية.

فلسفة الرقص - ص 40

نعم، أيها القارئ، لقد قرأت بشكل صحيح: ما هو على المحك في هذا النص -بخجل وكما لو كان خفيًا- هو شعر عام لفعل الكائنات الحية. وكان هذا بالفعل معنى هذه الملاحظة غير الضارة تقريبًا حيث حدد في قلب الرقص شيئًا ما باعتباره "طريقة للحياة الباطنية ، عبر إعطاء هذا المصطلح النفسي الآن معنى جديدًا ليهيمن علم وظائف الأعضاء بمجرد أن نتوقف عن فصل العقل عن الجسد، يظهر الرقص والفكر على حقيقتهما: نفس الشيء. يعني شعر عام.

فاليري — ويبدو أنه ظل فريدًا في هذا حتى الآن — يعتبر هنا أن ديناميكيات الفنون والفكر هي النشاط الأساسي، ليس لإنسانية غريبة عن الطبيعة — وكما لو أنها سقطت من السماء — بل للنشاط الأساسي. للمملكة الحية بأكملها

www.ingramcontent.com/pod-product-compliance
Lightning Source LLC
Chambersburg PA
CBHW030405160726
47992CB00007B/2972